COMPLETE CONDITIONING FOR RUGBY

Dan Luger
Paul Pook

Human Kinetics

Library of Congress Cataloging-in-Publication Data

Luger, Dan, 1975-
  Complete conditioning for rugby / Dan Luger, Paul Pook.
    p. cm.
  ISBN 0-7360-5210-0 (Soft cover)
  1. Rugby football—Training.   I. Pook, Paul.   II. Title.
  GV945.8.L84 2004
  796.333—dc22   2003023734

ISBN: 0-7360-5210-0

Copyright © 2004 by Dan Luger and Paul Pook

Acquisitions Editor: Ed McNeely; **Developmental Editor:** Leigh LaHood; **Assistant Editor:** Kim Thoren; **Copyeditor:** Nancy Elgin; **Proofreader:** Erin Cler; **Permission Manager:** Toni Harte; **Graphic Designer:** Nancy Rasmus; **Graphic Artist:** Sandra Meier; **Photo Manager:** Dan Wendt; **Cover Designer:** Keith Blomberg; **Photographer (cover):** © David Rogers/Getty Images; **Photographer (interior):** Sportsbeat Images; **Art Manager:** Kareema McLendon; **Illustrators:** Roberto Sabas (line drawings) and Kareema McLendon (drill diagrams); **Printer:** United Graphics

Human Kinetics books are available at special discounts for bulk purchase. Special editions or book excerpts can also be created to specification. For details, contact the Special Sales Manager at Human Kinetics.

Printed in the United States of America   10 9 8 7 6 5 4 3 2 1

Human Kinetics
Web site: www.HumanKinetics.com

United States: Human Kinetics
P.O. Box 5076
Champaign, IL 61825-5076
800-747-4457
e-mail: humank@hkusa.com

Canada: Human Kinetics
475 Devonshire Road Unit 100
Windsor, ON N8Y 2L5
800-465-7301 (in Canada only)
e-mail: orders@hkcanada.com

Europe: Human Kinetics
107 Bradford Road
Stanningley
Leeds LS28 6AT, United Kingdom
+44 (0) 113 255 5665
e-mail: hk@hkeurope.com

Australia: Human Kinetics
57A Price Avenue
Lower Mitcham, South Australia 5062
08 8277 1555
e-mail: liaw@hkaustralia.com

New Zealand: Human Kinetics
Division of Sports Distributors NZ Ltd.
P.O. Box 300 226 Albany
North Shore City
Auckland
0064 9 448 1207
e-mail: blairc@hknewz.com

CONTENTS

PREFACE

When I first joined Harlequins in 1996—the year after rugby first became a professional sport—the club coaches put me through a number of tests to assess my fitness. I thought I was pretty sharp, but they took me aside.

"Luger," they said, "your strength and speed are fantastic, but you don't have the aerobic conditioning and cardiovascular fitness that the game at this level will demand." They gave me a program to follow, and I enthusiastically went to work on developing my conditioning the way they prescribed.

"Luger," they said eight weeks later, "your aerobic fitness is excellent, but you've lost your strength and speed!"

I felt a little like we were fumbling around in the dark, going around in circles trying to get me in top condition. From that time on, I made it my business to find out from the experts what approaches to training would make me perform better on match day.

Eight years later, I still haven't stopped looking. I have realized that you never stop learning. The point at which you convince yourself that you're the finished article is the point where you stop improving.

Rugby has gone through tumultuous change in recent years as we have pushed to become more competitive at all levels. A new, results-oriented culture has grown from a hotbed of ideas and analysis. Where once there was a shortage of people who understood physical performance, now experts share with each other knowledge characterized by both its depth and quality.

As well as thanking Paul Pook, whose expertise and enthusiasm know no bounds whatever the challenge, I would also like to mention Margo Wells, who was enlightening and a source of inspiration, the Rugby Football Union's Dave Reddin, and the Beastmaster himself, Tony Lester. Each has had a major part to play in helping me reach for the next level of performance.

In my experience, a personalized, specific approach to conditioning for rugby works on both the individual and team levels. If you assess what you need to do on the pitch to succeed—if you fine-tune your strengths and eradicate your weaknesses—you can enhance your selection prospects, play up to your potential, and contribute to your team's success.

That you're reading this book indicates that you want to improve your own or your team's performance. You are part of the new rugby culture and realize that at whatever level you are competing, success depends heavily on your attitude toward and approach to complete conditioning.

I am convinced that you will benefit from reading this book and practicing the drills, strategies, and programs it presents. It will not happen overnight, but if you train hard and smart, the rewards will come. It's simple and specific, and it works for me.

Dan Luger

ACKNOWLEDGMENTS

We dedicate this book to Nick Duncombe, a great friend and talented player who died suddenly at the age of 21. Nick, you will always be an inspiration to us.

Our thanks go to Dave Williams of Big Bug Sports for his much valued support and guidance. We also thank Nicki Jupp for her excellent feedback and modeling of the drills.

INTRODUCTION

The approach to rugby conditioning has undergone a revolution since the sport went professional in 1995. As players have become faster, stronger, and more athletic, their skill levels have improved, and the game has become more dynamic and popular with spectators as a result. Although its importance was not always appreciated, conditioning is now a central component of preparation for rugby. Top players follow comprehensive and varied training programs based on the latest research, the demands of the game, and their individual and positional playing needs.

The aim of this book is to convey recent training and coaching developments—including the latest drills and strategies—as they are used by today's rugby athletes and coaches. A range of exercises for different levels of fitness and skill are presented for each element of rugby conditioning. Choosing drills and designing a program that meets your specific requirements allow you to develop the movement patterns and energy systems required for high-speed rugby.

Coaches, players, and sport scientists have recently addressed several key issues regarding conditioning for rugby. We'll summarize their conclusions.

1. **Endurance training.** Traditionally, there has been too much emphasis on aerobic training. Rugby is a power sport that relies on a high level of anaerobic (without oxygen) energy. Almost all rugby movements demand that strong forces be produced in short periods of time, as when making a tackle, jumping to catch a ball, or pushing in the scrum, and the aerobic system is simply too slow to fuel these activities. Sound aerobic conditioning is still very important for rugby players, but it ought to be developed through fuel mix conditioning (drills that require a mixture of aerobic and anaerobic fuels) and not overemphasized at the expense of strength, speed, and power development.

2. **Functional training.** The term *functional training* stresses the need to train in the same way that you play—in multiple planes of movement and involving acceleration, deceleration, and stabilization. This approach also highlights the need to train specific movements, not muscles,

and is proving to be more effective than older methods for improving rugby performance and preventing injury.

3. **Core stability.** Core stability is a fundamental element of functional training. It is defined as the ability of the trunk to support the efforts and forces of the arms and legs so that muscles and joints can perform in their safest, strongest, and most effective positions. In rugby terms, you become more stable in contact, better able to withstand tackling, and less likely to experience injuries involving the lower back. In a nutshell, your body can function more effectively with less risk.

4. **Strength training.** Strength training for rugby has tended to emphasize bodybuilding and training muscles rather than movements, resulting in players who have increased their size but not necessarily their rugby-specific strength. Training has also tended to focus on "mirror dominant" muscles like the biceps, pectorals, and quadriceps—the muscles that are clearly seen in the mirror. As a result, rugby players often exhibit the following characteristics:

• Overdeveloped chest muscles, but rounded and unstable shoulders result from excessive bench pressing and too few pulling and shoulder-stability exercises.

• Overdeveloped upper abdominal muscles and hip flexors result from concentrating on traditional sit-ups and crunches, resulting in tight hip flexors, excessive curve in the lower back, and a forward tilt to the pelvis, which produce poor posture, lower-back pain, and greater susceptibility to hamstring and groin injuries.

• Overdeveloped upper-body strength relative to lower-body strength leads to muscular imbalances and poor-quality movement. The legs must generate a strong propulsive force for virtually all rugby movements, including tackling, changing direction, and driving play. Strength training for the lower body therefore is a fundamental component of complete conditioning for rugby.

In *Complete Conditioning for Rugby*, we focus on developing the fundamental strength needed for the movement skills of rugby. This approach to conditioning teaches the appropriate muscles to fire and control movement so they are strong when you move forward to, for example, hit a ruck; strong in rotation, as when you maul a ball; and strong during deceleration, like when you stop sharply.

5. **Injury prevention.** Prioritizing within the conditioning program the techniques that aid in injury prevention is of growing importance. Injury rates in rugby are on the rise as the ball stays in play longer and increasingly powerful and heavy players produce higher-impact collisions and greater running intensities. Other factors, including poor

methods of conditioning, muscle imbalances, and weak stabilizing muscles, also increase injuries. The functional approach to conditioning that we advocate throughout *Complete Conditioning for Rugby* is designed to reduce the likelihood of injuries while enhancing performance. Following the warm-up drills and recovery strategies discussed in chapters 4 and 9 can also reduce injury rates.

Complete Conditioning for Rugby explores these issues and new ideas in 10 easy-to-follow chapters. Chapter 1 highlights the demands of rugby and provides useful information on how these requirements dictate complete conditioning. Chapter 2 covers the key training principles that provide a framework for systematic training, whereas chapter 3 sets out methods for testing rugby fitness to teach you to assess and monitor your level of rugby-specific conditioning.

Chapters 4, 5, 6, and 7 catalog over 100 drills for enhancing strength, power, speed, and agility and include strategies for warming up effectively. The diversity of the drills within these sections allows you to add variety to your training program and to select exercises suitable for your level of conditioning. To ensure your safety and maximize improvement, we encourage you to focus on technique and control when performing all conditioning drills.

Guidelines and drills for improving fuel mix conditioning for both individuals and teams are presented in chapter 8. These drills improve the players' capacity to generate energy and resist fatigue so they can perform effectively for the duration of the game. Traditionally, fuel mix training has been called *endurance* or *stamina training,* but these terms suggest that rugby is an aerobic sport. We prefer to use the term *fuel mix* to emphasize the simultaneous contributions of anaerobic and aerobic energy during competitive rugby.

Strategies to help in recovering from training and competing are discussed in chapter 9. Now regarded as a training principle, recovery is an integral part of the training program. This chapter advises players and coaches on formulating guidelines and strategies to minimize fatigue and restore energy. Nutrition and the role of food and fluid in sustaining performance are also considered. Guidelines given at the end of this chapter will help you to optimize your nutrition plan.

Chapter 10 integrates all the elements of conditioning to guide you through the process of designing your own training programs. We provide typical in- and off-season programs for professional and amateur players, including programs for three players who have different conditioning profiles and training targets.

Adhering to the guidelines and perfecting the drills set out in *Complete Conditioning for Rugby* will allow you to train intelligently and ensure that you get the most from your training program.

CHAPTER 1

FITNESS DEMANDS OF RUGBY

When we watch a rugby match,

the efforts and skills of the players impress us, but we tend to focus on how many tries are scored and the result of the match. Most of us agree that we could never equal the 100-meter or marathon records set by elite athletes, but do we appreciate the challenges that face the rugby athlete? In the space of an 80-minute game, an international flanker may make 25 tackles, hit 46 rucks, push during 22 scrums, and lift during 24 lineouts. Players typically cover distances of six to eight kilometers at varying running speeds separated into over 200 intervals of varying distances. This requires strength, power, speed, agility, and an ability to repeat and recover from movements for the duration of the game. Obviously, elite rugby players face unique conditioning challenges.

By analyzing competitive rugby, we can qualify and quantify the typical movement patterns that players engage in. This crucial information, presented in this chapter, allows us to predict the energy demands of the sport and assess the specific strength and power activities used, as well as their frequency. Knowledge of these facts is essential to designing effective conditioning programs for players.

CHANGING DEMANDS OF RUGBY

Game play has changed greatly over the past two decades. Now, the ball is in play longer, rest time between cycles of play is shorter, and players make considerably more passes and tackles during a game. A comparison of two of the most entertaining games of the former and current eras, Scotland versus Wales in 1971 and Australia versus New Zealand in 2000, shows just how much the game has evolved (see table 1.1).

These statistics show that play is more continuous, with fewer stoppages and longer cycles of play. Today's rugby player is expected to run and handle the ball much more with less rest. Less time is spent performing scrums and lineout set piece plays. A study on defensive play (Harrigan, T. and M. Hughes, 2002, *Defensive play in elite men's rugby union,* Centre for Performance Analysis, UWIC, Cardiff) also shows that teams are making almost twice as many tackles during a game (an average of 86 per team) as were made during the 1996 Five Nations Championships (when the average was 48 tackles per team).

Players' average body weight has also changed. Table 1.2 contrasts the average weight of All Black outside backs in 1973 and 1999. This clearly

Table 1.1   Statistical Comparison of Scotland Versus Wales, 1971, and Australia Versus New Zealand, 2000

	Scotland vs. Wales, 1971	Australia vs. New Zealand, 2000
Ball in play (min.:s.)	24:34 (31%)	34:17 (43%)
Stoppages	151	68
Lineouts	71	18
Scrums	39	14
Kicks in open play	85	36
Passes	145	325
Cycles over 30 s.	3 (7%)	27 (40%)

C. Thomas, © International Rugby Board, 2003.

Table 1.2   Player Body Weight Comparison, 1973 and 1999

	Average weight, 1973 (kg)	Average weight, 1999 (kg)
Outside half	74.4	86.3
Center	81.8	98.8
Wing	80	102.3
Fullback	80	86

C. Thomas, © International Rugby Board, 2003.

indicates that the physicality of the game has developed over a quarter of a century. In addition to today's emphasis on strength and power training—which has increased muscle mass and, therefore, body weight—rugby now attracts athletes who are naturally bigger and more powerful, and they tend to make successful rugby players. There are obvious exceptions to this rule, but whether you are Jonah Lomu or Austin Healey, in today's games you have to train to be prepared for heavier, more intense collisions.

MOVEMENT PATTERNS AND CONDITIONING

Analyzing the movements of rugby helps to illustrate the varying demands placed on rugby players. We will now summarize how these demands make specific elements of conditioning necessary and provide a pathway for designing playing-position-specific conditioning programs.

Rugby can be broken down into a series of movement patterns separated by intervals of running at varying speeds, including walking, jogging, half- and three-quarters-pace running, and maximal sprinting. Conditioning programs for contemporary rugby players have to address these and other factors so that players can meet the demands of the sport and avoid injury. These movement patterns include

- making and breaking tackles;
- scrummaging;
- jumping in a lineout;
- lifting in a lineout;

- driving a maul;
- passing and catching;
- kicking out of hand;
- kicking for a goal;
- hitting rucks;
- ripping the ball;
- off-loading in contact;
- getting up from the ground; and
- accelerating, decelerating, and quickly changing direction.

Strength and Power

Strength and power drills, discussed in chapter 6, are probably the most important forms of conditioning for rugby because they prepare players for the demanding collisions and multidirectional movements of the game and reduce the likelihood of injury.

Tackling, being tackled, rucking, and mauling all involve maximal efforts that challenge a player's strength and power. Training for these movements includes muscle-stability and muscle-control drills to help support the joints during impacts, with particular emphasis to be placed on the key stabilizers of the trunk, which brace the spine and support the efforts of the arms and legs during all rugby movements. This functional approach to strength training helps players in moving forward to hit a ruck, for example; in rotating, such as when mauling a ball; and in decelerating to stop sharply.

Power drills improve a player's ability to produce explosive movement patterns like tackling, jumping, accelerating, and bursting through tacklers. These drills are covered in chapter 6.

Fuel Mix Conditioning

Players rely heavily on fuel mix conditioning to enable them to repeat movement patterns and to aid in recovery. Movements such as tackling and rucking must be performed too rapidly for the aerobic system to supply enough energy to the muscles, so anaerobic fuel powers these movements. The aerobic system promotes recovery between dynamic movements and fuels less-intense activities like walking and jogging. A

Table 1.3   Varying Running Intensities by Position and Tackle and Ruck Counts During a 2003 International Rugby Match

	Prop	Flanker	Fly half	Center	Wing
Sprinting (min.:s.)	0:00	0:03	0:27	0:19	0:31
High-speed running (min.:s.)	0:27	1:08	2:36	1:25	1:44
Running (min.:s.)	5:35	5:56	5:10	3:36	3:42
Jogging (min.:s.)	16:06	13:36	14:34	14:45	12:42
Walking (min.:s.)	56:38	51:10	47:21	54:45	57:01
Tackles	15	25	15	12	9
Rucks	40	46	22	22	16

Courtesy of RFU, 2003.

breakdown of these activities and their frequency during international-level competition is provided in table 1.3.

Figures 1.1 and 1.2 represent the heart rate of a fly half and back-row forward, respectively, during an international match. The curves represent the two 40-minute halves of the game and the halftime. The average heart rate during the first half for the fly half is 158 beats per minute compared to 175 beats per minute for the back-row forward. Both of these averages represent high work rate, particularly for the back-row

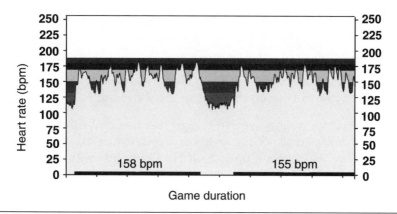

Figure 1.1   Fly half's heart rate curve.
Data from Peter Herbert.

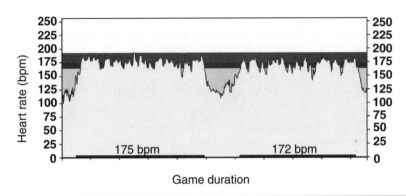

Figure 1.2   Back-row forward's heart rate curve.
Data from Peter Herbert.

forward. This player also reaches heart rates greater than 85 percent of maximal heart rate on a regular basis, illustrating a very high work rate. The fluctuations in heart rate represented by the "up and down" nature of the heart rate curves also highlight the start-and-stop nature of rugby.

Heart rate may also be monitored during fuel mix or rugby training drills to assess the level of a player's work rate and recovery during these sessions. This information can inform the player and coach of the demands of the session and help design sessions that provoke similar heart rate responses to those experienced during competition.

Another set of reliable statistics that informs the design of fuel mix drills involves the amount of time that the ball is in play. During competitive rugby matches at a professional level, the ball is in play for 25 to 35 minutes, consisting of cycles of play separated by periods of rest.

- Most cycles of continuous play last an average of 23 seconds.
- The typical range of cycles is 5 to 63 seconds.
- Rest periods vary in length, with the average being 42 seconds.
- The longest periods of rest occur after tries, penalty kicks at goal, or when a player is receiving treatment for an injury.

With this information, we can design fuel mix drills that mimic the work and rest periods of competition. Specific fuel mix drills should therefore involve varying periods of both high-intensity exercise and active rest time.

General fuel mix drills should also be included to build endurance before progressing to more rugby-specific anaerobic drills. Endurance drills are performed at a lower intensity and rely on greater contributions from the aerobic system.

Speed and Agility

It is vital that players' speed and agility be developed. While running at high or maximal speeds, players will cover distances ranging from 3 to 34 meters. This often involves changing direction, acting as a support player, making or breaking a tackle, or hitting a ruck. The average high-speed run for forwards and halfbacks spans about 8 meters, whereas centers, wings, and fullbacks average closer to 16 meters. Running also includes backward and lateral movements, such as retreating to avoid the offside line, shadowing an attacker, or evading opponents during a lineout. These statistics confirm that rugby relies heavily on acceleration—the capacity to rapidly reach a high speed from various starting positions—supported by agility, which is the ability to change direction and decelerate quickly. Drills that develop these qualities are described in chapter 7.

Centers, wings, and fullbacks also sprint over greater distances than other team members, so basic speed drills must be included in their training program to extend speed beyond the acceleration phase.

POSITIONAL DIFFERENCES

Statistics clearly show that distinctive demands are placed on team members according to their playing positions. For example, the prop's role in a game is vastly different from that of a winger. During the 2003 international match outlined in table 1.3, the prop was involved in 40 energy-sapping rucks and made 15 tackles, whereas the winger—the author of this book—only hit 16 rucks and made 9 tackles, which was significantly less than my teammates in other positions. However, I reached sprinting speed for a total of 31 seconds over 12 intervals, the highest figure for the team.

Of key importance in determining conditioning needs are the work rates (represented by the number of tackles, rucks, and set piece plays a player participates in) of forwards and backs. These figures demonstrate that wingers need to concentrate their training on developing speed and speed endurance, whereas forwards should focus on aerobic fitness and fuel mix conditioning. The elevated work rates of props, hookers, and second- and back-row forwards make it necessary for them to engage in more fuel mix conditioning than is required for backs. Forwards must also have good strength and stability to meet the demands of frequent scrummaging, mauling, rucking, and tackling.

LEVEL OF COMPETITION AND CONDITIONING DEMANDS

A comparison of international and professional club games during 2003 illustrates considerable differences in play at these two levels of competition. The ball was in play for significantly longer in international games—sometimes for more than 40 minutes—compared to an average of 31 minutes during club games. Running speed statistics were similar at the two levels, but significantly more tackles were made in international matches.

The ball-in-play time at an amateur level is closer to 23 minutes. When the ball is in play for less time during a game, fewer tackles, rucks, and set piece plays are performed and less time is spent running. Movement patterns are also performed with less dynamism at the club level, although the players' level of effort is probably the same as that of the elite players. This illustrates that the higher the level of competition, the greater the conditioning demands on the player.

MENTAL TOUGHNESS

Some top rugby players exhibit a certain psychological quality that has helped them excel. All Black legend Zinzan Brooke defines this quality—mental toughness—as "an attitude or a quality that I've always had. It's what I call this 'mongrel streak' in me that means once I bite something, I want to hold on and just not drop it." Determination, aggression, self-confidence, and self-discipline are all qualities that players need to succeed in rugby, and developing these mental skills can also be incorporated into player and team conditioning regimens.

Dan's Top Tip

I have a switch at the back of my mind. It's a psychological switch I flip on when my ability to rise to a challenge or achieve something is questioned.

When I turn the switch on, I affirm to myself that I've got what it takes to succeed and that nothing will stop me. I call up mental pictures of similar situations that I've dealt with successfully to back up my confidence. I keep reminding myself of my role and purpose until they're firmly in my mind.

So, when you're faced with a challenge—whether it's rehab after a major injury, the last big set of weighted push-ups, the disappointment of not being selected for a starting place on the team, or going for a win when you're down by seven points with only three minutes left on the clock—turn on the switch in your head, silently affirm "You'll never beat me," and you'll know you can take anything that's thrown at you!

TEAM SPIRIT

Team spirit in rugby involves teammates respecting and trusting each other and sharing the enjoyment of working toward common goals. It is not a simple concept or easy to achieve, but when it flourishes it fosters commitment and increases the chances of winning.

British Lions flanker Richard Hill talked about his team's spirit—and the winning edge it gave them—following the Lions' successful tour to South Africa in 1997. The main reason the Lions beat the Springboks, Hill said, was "because we became a team in the true sense of the word; we understood each other, we had respect for each other, we had a deep sense of common purpose."

SKILLS AND TACTICS

Optimizing your conditioning will help you perform better and keep your skill level consistently high throughout a match. It is no surprise that during the last quarter of most games is when both scoring rates and the number of mistakes—missed tackles, handling errors, bad decisions—are the highest, as the heart diverts oxygenated blood from the brain to the failing muscles.

It is important to incorporate handling and positional skills in conditioning drills to maximize training time. Warm-up in particular should include passing and catching drills, and fuel mix drills should incorporate rugby skills for maximum benefit. The majority of drills included in

Complete Conditioning for Rugby replicate and enhance rugby movement techniques.

Teams must have a strategy and general game plan for competitive play. Some teams are known for spreading the ball wide to the backs, whereas other teams are more conservative in their attack and kick for positioning before attempting to break down the opposition's defense. Sometimes, a team's strategy is related to its level of conditioning. Teams with high levels of fuel mix conditioning, for example, use that to their advantage by playing at a fast pace, reducing the time between set piece moves, and running the ball from their own half of the pitch. Teams that focus on strength and power in their conditioning may use runner after runner to try to break down a defense or keep feeding the ball to the forwards, who can gain territory with driving mauls. Teams may also adapt their style of play to the opposition or weather conditions.

PLANNING THE CONDITIONING PROGRAM

In summary, players and coaches must adopt the unique blend of conditioning elements that will allow their team to play successfully and without injury. The chapters in this book address each of these elements, as well as recognized training principles, methods of fitness testing, and strategies for promoting flexibility, posture, recovery, and optimum nutrition.

No matter what your level of competition, your conditioning philosophy should be the same as that of players at all levels. The novice amateur player and skilled professional both require stability, strength, and power for making contact, speed and agility to chase attackers and evade defenders, and fuel mix conditioning to sustain these activities. Although amateur players may not achieve the level of conditioning of their elite counterparts, they will still benefit from the improved performance and resistance to injury that conditioning affords.

Junior players (ages 12 to 18 years) have different conditioning needs than adults do. Games at this level are played for 70 minutes, not 80, and scrums may not be pushed for more than 1.5 meters. Ironically, although the contact demands placed on players are the same as in adult play, stability and strength drills are frequently ignored at this age level. Body weight strength drills—including control and core stabilization drills—should be performed at this stage, but speed, agility, and fuel mix conditioning are less of an issue. These last three elements are best developed in players in this age range by participating in a number of sports, which they should be encouraged to do.

CHAPTER 2

PRINCIPLES OF RUGBY TRAINING

Training principles are an essential component of a systematic approach to conditioning for rugby. These established, yet continually evolving, principles provide the framework on which a safe and effective training program is developed and monitored. The purpose of conditioning is to induce in players specific adaptations that will improve their performance in all of the elements of conditioning, including strength, endurance, and speed. Players are more likely to achieve these changes if their training program adheres to these underlying principles:

- Injury prevention
- Specificity
- Overload
- Periodization
- Enjoyment

INJURY PREVENTION

It's almost impossible to avoid certain injuries caused by impact during rugby, although improved conditioning and technique may reduce the likelihood. However, a large percentage of the injuries that players sustain do not involve impact. Lower-back problems, hamstring strain, and tendon inflammation are just a few of the injuries that often result from having poor technique or weak stabilizing muscles, or from simply failing to warm up correctly. Most soft-tissue injuries can be avoided by adhering to injury prevention strategies and a well-designed conditioning program. A number of principles and drills that help to prevent injury are covered in *Complete Conditioning for Rugby:*

- Take a functional approach to training that develops strength in various planes of movement by using, for example, rotational medicine ball drills, deceleration drills, and drills that mimic the movement patterns of rugby.

- Include drills that enhance muscle and joint stability, such as balance drills, core stability drills, and control drills.

- Progress from a focus on stabilization to strength and power training.

- Incorporate fuel mix drills to help players build resistance to fatigue, which is a key cause of rugby injuries.

- Design training programs based on an informed analysis of the demands of playing rugby.

- Respect the importance of flexibility and posture.

- Begin each training session with appropriate warm-up exercises.

- Use recovery strategies such as cooling down, contrast bathing, and replacing fluids.

- Focus on using correct technique during all drills, such as explosive lifting.

- Individualize the training program and its conditioning targets and include appropriate fitness-testing protocols.

Introducing injury prevention strategies at an early age and reversing rugby's emphasis on injury rehabilitation rather than injury prevention will help players avoid their worst fear—getting injured.

> ### Dan's Top Tip

In 2001, I suffered a serious knee injury that threatened my career, but with the expertise of a top surgeon, a physiotherapist, and strength and conditioning coaches, I regained my fitness and returned to topflight rugby. During my rehabilitation, I performed specific strengthening exercises, balance drills, and proprioceptive plyometric drills (jumping in various directions) that challenged and developed my knees' stability. Recently, my teammates integrated these drills into their own training programs even though they don't have knee problems. This approach is called *prehabilitation* or *body protection*, which means that you perform specialized drills to prevent injury rather than wait for the injury to happen.

SPECIFICITY

The principle of *specificity* means that the conditioning elements used should be associated with the sport. Appropriate drills should be developed to help players successfully perform the movement patterns of competition. Of course, playing a match is the best way to enhance rugby conditioning, but to induce significant adaptation and prevent injury, the movement patterns and energy systems also need to be trained in isolation.

In the previous chapter, we identified for the various playing positions the typical movement patterns and energy-system contributions that should be targeted in the conditioning program. For example, at a professional level, back-row forwards make 10 to 20 tackles per game, so those players need to have a high level of explosive strength and the endurance to keep tackling for the duration of the game.

Most rugby activities—such as tackling, accelerating, and rucking—are fueled primarily by the anaerobic system with the support of the aerobic system. This simultaneous use of anaerobic and aerobic energy is called a *fuel mix*, and training programs must include fuel mix drills to develop the energy capacity for rugby. The traditional approach to improving energy provision for rugby has been nonspecific and often has involved excessive aerobic training, such as running at a constant pace for several miles. Although this form of training does improve aerobic fitness, it does not adhere to the principle of specificity for rugby because there is little or no fuel mix conditioning.

Cross-training drills such as cycling and rowing are also nonspecific because they do not mimic the movement patterns of rugby. However, they can be helpful in developing fuel mix conditioning early in a training program or when specific drills are not possible because of injury.

Specificity of drills in strength and power training develops strength in all planes of motion, including rotation, flexion, and extension. An example is the Turnover Ball—Squat and Pull drill, shown in figure 2.1, which requires the rapid production of strength, including rotation and extension, and mimics the pulling movement of mauling a ball from an opponent on the ground.

Specificity in strength and power training is important, but less-functional drills like the Bench Press also improve overall strength. However, these drills should not dominate the strength and power program.

In summary, specificity ensures that training helps as much as possible to prevent injury and enhance performance on the pitch. Conditioning should mimic the energy system use and movement patterns of rugby.

a   b

Figure 2.1   The Turnover Ball—Squat and Pull drill is an example of specificity, because it uses the same motion as mauling a ball from an opponent on the ground.

OVERLOAD

Physical conditioning is improved by subjecting the body to *overload*—demands that cause strain or fatigue. The goal is adaptation, and the body becomes better able to cope with challenges if overloading is gradual and improvements are monitored. If a player trains too hard or progresses too quickly, adaptation does not occur and performance is inhibited or, worse still, injury occurs. The same may happen if a player undertrains.

Note that adaptation and improvements in conditioning actually take place during rest following exercise, because it is the body's recovery from these stresses that makes it stronger, rather than the exercise itself. This highlights the importance of rest and management of overload.

The appropriate amount of overload depends on an individual's training status, injury history, and training background, all of which are aspects of a complete conditioning profile. These factors, plus the results of fitness tests, dictate the training goals and choice of training mode and provide a way to gauge progress. A slower rate of progression is needed for players who have a low level of conditioning and a less strenuous exercise history, whereas those with a strong conditioning background can progress more quickly.

The time of the rugby year at which the training is taking place also affects the amount of overload that should be applied. During the competitive season, excessive training must be avoided so players are fresh for games. The off- and preseasons are good times for overloading. The principle of periodization, discussed later in this chapter, deals with planning for optimal training and performance.

To apply the appropriate degrees of strain and fatigue to the body's nervous, muscular, and energy systems, load variables must be manipulated continually. These variables—namely exercise selection, intensity, frequency, rest, and volume—significantly affect adaptation.

Exercise Selection

Different forms of exercise place different types of overload on the body. For example, plyometrics is an excellent form of power training, but plyometric exercises should not be included in training until a certain level of stability and strength is present to minimize the risk of injury. Another example of appropriate exercise selection is to perform exercises with body weight before adding extra resistance. The appropriate exercise-selection strategy for progressive overload is simple to complex, stable to unstable, body weight to extra resistance, and low load to high load.

Intensity

Measures of intensity include the amount of the resistance load (often measured as a percentage of the individual's maximum), the height or distance jumped during plyometrics, or, in running, the percentage achieved of maximum heart rate or running speed. For example, in fuel mix conditioning, the relative contributions of aerobic and anaerobic fuels are directly related to the running intensity. The greater the running intensity, the greater the anaerobic contribution.

In all elements of conditioning, the overload intensity must be advanced to a level greater than that experienced during competition to prepare the player for the demands of the game.

Frequency and Rest

The period of rest after a bout of exercise affects the outcome of the activity that follows. For example, players must be given sufficient rest between sets of speed and agility drills to replenish their high-power anaerobic energy supply and allow the nervous system to recover so that the quality of their movement can be maintained. During resistance training, the length of the rest period can be modified to suit the physiological adaptation being sought. Relatively short rest periods of 30 to 60 seconds are used during hypertrophy sessions to stimulate growth hormone production, whereas rest periods of at least 3 minutes are needed for exercises stressing maximum strength or power development.

Volume

Volume refers to the total number of lifts or the total weight lifted during a resistance training session or to the distance covered during a speed training session. Training volume should be reduced from off- and preseason levels during the competition phase of the season, when increased rest is the better option.

PERIODIZATION

Periodization is the division of the training plan into phases or cycles with specific objectives. Conditioning for rugby is challenging because various fitness components must be developed and technical and tactical development must also be accommodated. Teams generally compete every 7 days for a period of more than 32 weeks, so correctly managing training overload by using periodization is crucial.

The most effective way to encourage physical adaptation is to focus during a training phase on specific elements of conditioning while also minimizing the loss of other elements. In the competitive season, for example, there are times when a general mix of training is beneficial. By dividing these phases into training blocks of three to six weeks, fitness components that complement each other can be emphasized. For example, training blocks that combine speed and strength drills or fuel mix conditioning and strength endurance work well, but speed and endurance training should not be combined because the level of general fatigue created by the endurance component does not support effective speed development.

Monitoring

The athlete's adaptive response to training must be measured to prevent under- and overtraining. Communicating with players is essential to the monitoring process and may include having them regularly assess their subjective feelings of tiredness or sharpness, supported by a battery of objective measurements of their physical and mental states. Examples of monitoring measures are provided in the chapters on Rugby Fitness Testing and Recovery and Nutrition.

The Rugby Year

The rugby year is split into four phases—active rest, off-season, preseason, and in-season—during which players can concentrate on various conditioning components and objectives. They are summarized in table 2.1.

However, it must be stressed that the emphasis in training depends on the individual's conditioning profile and should progress from core stabilization and general fuel mix drills to power, speed, agility, and specific fuel mix conditioning.

Active Rest

The active rest period starts as soon as the competitive season ends. It provides an opportunity to rest, regenerate, and address any fundamental conditioning deficiencies before embarking on a significant phase of conditioning in the off-season phase. This phase may last for two to eight

Table 2.1   The Four Phases of the Rugby Year

Phase	Number of weeks	Training drills and objectives
Active rest	2 to 8	Rest and recovery
		Corrective exercise and control drills
		Cross-training (tennis, cycling)
Off-season	4 to 6	Stability, pattern, and loaded strength drills
		General and specific fuel mix drills
		Speed and agility drills
Preseason	4 to 6	Power training drills
		Specific fuel mix drills
		Speed and agility drills
		Maintain stability and pattern strength abilities
In-season	32 to 36	Blocks of fuel mix, strength, and power training drills
		Speed and agility drills
		Maintain aspects of conditioning that are satisfactory and gradually improve weaknesses

weeks, according to the level and volume of in-season competition. Players who have played more than 28 games should allocate at least 4 weeks for this phase, while those who have missed games because of injury or deselection may opt for a shorter rest period. Although rest is vital, players should be encouraged to participate in cross-training or other sports such as swimming and tennis to help minimize the loss of general fitness and in corrective exercise to address muscle imbalances or injuries. Control strength drills are also of value during this phase.

Dan's Top Tip

Perform speed drills and short, sharp speed sessions year-round—even during the active rest phase. Short speed drills remind the muscles and joints of how to move quickly.

Off-Season

Because training increases in volume during the off-season, significant improvements in rugby conditioning should be made during this time. The player's conditioning profile (see chapter 3, Rugby Fitness Testing) is the template for setting the targets and focus of the training plan. The stage should begin with core stabilization and movement strength drills, then progress to specific fuel mix drills and loaded strength training. This provides a solid foundation for complete conditioning.

Preseason

Preseason training becomes increasingly specific to the activities performed during competitive rugby play. Many players complain that it is difficult to meet the conditioning demands of the first few fixtures (matches) of the in-season, and this usually results from emphasizing general fuel mix conditioning in the preseason phase at the expense of specific fuel mix training. Training in the preseason should concentrate on integrated circuit training and team conditioning games (see chapter 8) together with reactive speed and agility training (see chapter 7).

Technical and tactical training become prevalent in the preseason, reducing the time spent on conditioning. However, these sessions can also be used to develop specific fuel mix conditioning if the conditioning coach works closely with the technical coach. For example, playing touch or tag rugby and managing intensity and duration during rugby practices work on conditioning while technical and tactical skills are taught.

The preseason should end with "friendly fixtures," which help develop match fitness and body hardness and rehearse team tactics. At this point of the year, the best conditioning sessions are games!

In-Season

In-season conditioning is the most complex phase because a balance must be struck between technical and tactical training, conditioning, and recovery. Again, dedicated technical and tactical rugby sessions can be used to develop fuel mix conditioning, while blocks of strength, speed, and power drills should last for several weeks. It is not always necessary to adopt a maintenance approach to conditioning levels during the in-season. Match fitness improves as the season progresses, but some players may still need to improve aspects of their conditioning if they did not reach a satisfactory standard during the preseason phase.

ENJOYMENT

Despite its importance, enjoyment is rarely listed as a conditioning principle in textbooks and training guides. Rugby is primarily about playing, and players are motivated because they enjoy the game. Making rugby a professional sport increased the training demands and pressure placed on players to win, making a work-hard ethic even more important than it had been. Players and coaches must work hard to be successful, but conditioning and training for rugby should still be an enjoyable experience.

Strategies that foster enjoyment include

- using a positive and supportive coaching style;
- setting targets, because most players enjoy reaching for and meeting targets;
- varying conditioning drills by using the many exercises given in this book; and
- surprising players by substituting fun games such as rugby netball or soccer for the usual program.

The ability to design and employ enjoyable (yet demanding) training practices is a valuable coaching skill.

SUMMARY

Paying attention to training principles is an essential component of a systematic approach to conditioning for rugby. Adhering to these principles helps to protect players from injury and provides the basis for designing a training program. In a nutshell, training principles help rugby players train more effectively with less risk.

CHAPTER 3

RUGBY FITNESS TESTING

Monitoring and evaluating progress are integral parts of a conditioning program. Conditioning sessions provide feedback on performance (for example, the load lifted during a back squat reflects leg strength, and the time it takes to sprint 30 meters reflects speed), whereas rugby-related fitness tests measure the levels of conditioning and reconditioning after injury.

A formal fitness test can be administered at the beginning of a training program or phase and repeated periodically. All elements of conditioning should be measured to provide feedback for setting targets and designing the training program. Initial test results can be used to compare players and to identify their strengths and weaknesses. Periodic retests assess progress and provide information for manipulating the training program.

COMPLETE CONDITIONING PROFILE

Fitness testing is part of a complete conditioning profile that also incorporates other elements of assessment. A complete conditioning profile can include the following information:

- Training status—the type and volume of training the player has had
- Medical history—recurrent and long-term injuries, conditions such as asthma and diabetes
- Level of ambition—the player's aspirations in relation to rugby
- Exercise techniques—the techniques the player is familiar with, such as the lifting technique for loaded and Olympic lifts
- Feedback—the assessments of fellow players and coaches on training and performance
- Nutritional profile—the player's nutrient intake recorded in a food- and fluid-intake diary
- Match analysis—the number of games played, average tackle count, number of rucks hit, errors made, and number of meters covered at specific running speeds (the measurement of which requires special software)
- Mental toughness—an assessment of the player's mental skills by a sport psychologist and an appropriate mental training plan
- Muscle lengths, imbalances, and mechanics

Although this chapter deals specifically with fitness testing, we recommend that you consider all of the elements in a complete conditioning profile, as given in the list. The more detailed the conditioning profile, the more specific, individualized, and beneficial the conditioning program will be.

TEST ADMINISTRATION

Before you subject players to a battery of fitness tests, each player should complete a medical history questionnaire and give their informed consent for testing. Players should be in a rested state, with no residual fatigue from training. Appropriate warm-ups must be done before each test, and the tests should be clearly described before starting.

The two main principles of testing are reliability and specificity. Reliability is the degree to which a test consistently reproduces a given result. For example, counting the number of tackles made in a game as a gauge of fuel mix conditioning is not a reliable test because so many variables affect how many tackles are made. A test must have set parameters and be administered in exactly the same way each time for it to be a consistent gauge of performance. For example, a three-kilometer time trial must be repeated on the same track in similar weather conditions each time.

Specificity is the extent to which a test relates to rugby and the demands of the game. A rowing time trial is an inappropriate fuel mix test for rugby because rowing does not relate to the movement patterns of rugby. Inappropriate tests cannot correctly predict conditioning for rugby. The Running Clock Drill (described later in this chapter) is a specific fuel mix performance test because it challenges the energy systems in a manner that is similar to competitive rugby. The ultimate test of complete conditioning, of course, is how players perform during competition; fitness testing is a useful tool, but it cannot replicate the mental and physical demands of the game.

TAILORING THE PROGRAM

The way in which the information gathered during testing is analyzed and communicated to the player will determine whether it has a positive or negative effect on motivation. The player and coach need to agree on realistic short- and long-term targets that can be effectively measured by future testing. An objective goal might be simply to improve the score each time a test is performed.

FUEL MIX CONDITIONING TESTS

THREE-KILOMETER RUN

Purpose: To measure the aerobic element of fuel mix conditioning. Several national teams use this test on a regular basis (see target times and ratings in tables 3.1, 3.2, and 3.3). It is most appropriate for forwards, who require high levels of aerobic fitness, and for players who have a short training history or are returning after an injury. Players can perform the test in small, position-specific groups to encourage competition.

Table 3.1   Three-Kilometer Ratings for Amateur Male Rugby Players by Position (min.:s.)

	Poor	Fair	Good	Very good	Excellent
Front row	15:40+	<15:40	<14:30	<14:00	<13:30
Second row	15:15+	<15:15	<14:15	<13:30	<12:50
Back row	14:30+	<14:30	<13:20	<12:50	<12:10
Inside back	14:20+	<14:20	<13:30	<12:40	<12:00
Outside back	14:30+	<14:30	<13:50	<12:50	<12:20

Table 3.2   Three-Kilometer Ratings for Amateur Female Rugby Players by Position (min.:s.)

	Poor	Fair	Good	Very good	Excellent
Front row	18:20+	<18:20	<17:30	<16:40	<15:35
Second row	18:00+	<18:00	<16:50	<15:40	<14:55
Back row	17:10+	<17:10	<16:20	<15:30	<14:45
Halfback	17:00+	<17:00	<16:10	<15:30	<14:45
Outside back	16:30+	<16:30	<16:00	<15:20	<14:30

Table 3.3   Three-Kilometer Performance Targets for Male and Female International Rugby Players by Position (min.:s.)

Position	Male	Female
Prop	12:00	15:00
Hooker	11:45	14:00
Second row	11:55	14:15
Loose forward	11:30	13:00
Halfback	11:15	12:45
Center	11:30	13:00
Wing	11:50	13:30
Fullback	11:40	13:00

Equipment and area: 400-meter running track, stopwatch.

Procedure

1. Record the names of the participants on the test recording sheet.
2. Inform the players that three kilometers is seven and one-half laps around the track, and that the aim is to cover the distance as quickly as possible.
3. After each lap, call out to each player the distance remaining to avoid confusion.
4. Record each finish time in minutes and seconds.
5. Encourage players to walk a lap after the test to cool down.

RUNNING CLOCK DRILL

Purpose: To assess specific fuel mix conditioning. The test challenges a player's ability to perform high-intensity activity with short recovery periods and is a good indicator of fuel mix conditioning for rugby.

Repetitions of the Running Clock Drill are performed on a multidirectional course separated by rest periods of lengths determined by the amount of time taken to perform a repetition and the time registered on a running clock. The total time needed to complete all of the repetitions (see table 3.4) is the test score. A fatigue index is also calculated by subtracting the first lap time (set A) from the final lap time (set E).

The test should be performed at maximum intensity. In contrast with players with higher levels of fuel mix conditioning, players with poor levels will take more time to complete the drill and have a greater fatigue index.

Equipment and area: Grassy area of a minimum of 10 by 30 meters, measuring tape, fourteen poles, two stopwatches, and two coaches.

Procedure

1. Perform one lap of the course as part of your warm-up to familiarize yourself with the test (see steps 2 through 6 for course details).

2. Stand at the start line between poles P1 and P2, facing forward (that is, looking down the length of the course).

3. On the start command, shuffle (run laterally) left to P4, backpedal from P4 to P5, shuffle right to P6, and perform a down-up (bend knees, put hands to ground, extend legs, lower chest to ground, and get back up) behind and between P6 and P7.

4. Sprint straight and then around P8, P9, and P10 and through P11 and P12 to P13 and P14. Turn around and perform a down-up behind and between P13 and P14.

5. Sprint to between P11 and P12 (one foot must cross imaginary line made by P11 and P12), then back to P13 and P14 and perform another down-up behind the poles.

6. Sprint to the finish line between P1 and P3.

7. Steps 1 through 6 equal one lap of the Running Clock Drill course. When multiple laps are to be performed, immediately run around P1 after crossing the finish line and repeat the course, shuffling from the start line to P4.

8. The running clock's time dictates when you start each set and the rest time between sets.

Monitoring

1. Coaches must ensure that players correctly perform the down-ups (so that the chest touches the ground) and turn behind the imaginary lines between the poles. Players must not touch the poles during the test.

2. Start both stopwatches when the player begins the course. Table 3.4 details the running clock times for the test. Once the player completes set A (one lap), one stopwatch is stopped to record the

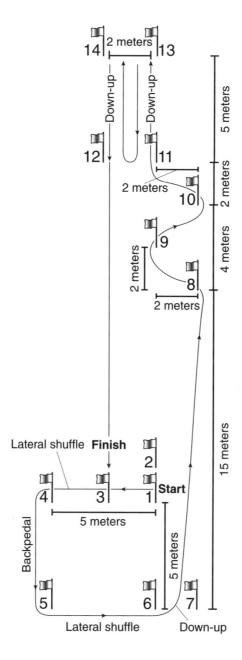

finish time of, for example, 25 seconds. The second watch is the running clock, and its time dictates the start time of subsequent sets. For example, if a player completes set A in 25 seconds, he rests for 35 seconds until the start time of set B—60 seconds.

3. Record the times to a tenth of a second for each set and add the times together at the end to get the test score. See standard ratings in table 3.5.

Table 3.4 Running Clock Drill Times

Running clock time (min.:s.)	Set/number of laps	Estimated set time (min.:s.)	Estimated rest time between sets (min.:s.)
0	A/1	0:23 to 0:33	0:27 to 0:37
1:00	B/2	0:55 to 1:05	0:55 to 1:05
3:00	C/1	0:24 to 0:34	0:26 to 0:36
4:00	D/3	1:25 to 1:55	0:45 to 1:05
6:30	E/1	0:25 to 0:35	

Table 3.5 Running Clock Drill Ratings for Professional Male Rugby Players by Position (min.:s.)

	Poor	Fair	Good	Very good	Excellent
Front row	4:25+	<4:25	<4:10	<4:00	<3:50
Second row	4:15+	<4:15	<4:05	<3:55	<3:45
Back row	4:10+	<4:10	<4:00	<3:50	<3:40
Back	4:05+	<4:05	<3:50	<3:40	<3:30

SPEED AND AGILITY TESTS

TEN- AND THIRTY-METER ACCELERATION TESTS

Purpose: To measure 10- and 30-meter sprint times. This test is relevant for all positions and reflects players' acceleration performance for rugby. Sprint tests are also useful for measuring reconditioning after rehabilitation of an injury. If a player's sprint times are significantly slower than they were originally (by 15 percent or more), the player should continue reconditioning rather than returning to competition.

Equipment and area: Measured track or 50 meters of flat running surface, electronic sprint timing gates (preferably touch-pad start) or stopwatch.

Procedure

1. Warm up thoroughly.
2. Start with one hand and the opposite foot on the start line. If using a touch pad, your lead hand must be on the pad. Start when you are ready.
3. Sprint as quickly as possible for 30 meters. During the sprint, the time taken to cover 10 meters is recorded; the 30-meter time is also recorded.
4. Perform three trials, taking time for a full recovery between each trial. Your best times are your scores.

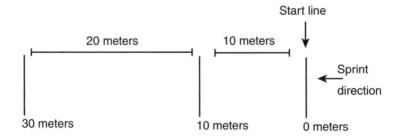

FLYING 30-METER SPEED TEST

Purpose: To measure basic speed after the acceleration phase. The test is appropriate for centers and outside backs.

Equipment and area: Measured track or 50 meters of flat running surface, six cones, and electronic sprint timing gates or stopwatch.

Procedure

1. Note that the test times the final 30 meters of the sprint, not the full distance.

2. Start with one hand and the opposite foot on the start line. Go when you are ready.

3. Sprint as quickly as possible for 50 meters. The time taken to cover the final 30 meters is recorded.

4. Perform three trials, taking time for a full recovery between each trial. The best time is your score.

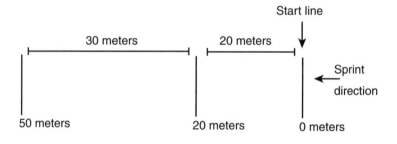

T TEST

Purpose: To measure speed and agility. This test is appropriate for all players. It measures the time taken to complete a course that includes forward, lateral, and backward running.

Equipment and area: Grass or indoor surface of 10 square meters, four cones, stopwatch or electronic sprint timing gates, and two coaches.

Procedure

1. Warm up thoroughly.

2. Start with one hand and the opposite foot on the start line. If a touch pad is used, your lead hand must be on the pad. If beams are used, the start line should be one meter behind the actual test distance start line. Start when you are ready.

3. From cone A, sprint forward to cone B and touch the base of it with your right hand.

4. Facing forward and not crossing your feet, shuffle left to cone C and touch its base with your left hand.

5. Shuffle 10 meters to cone D and touch its base with your right hand.

6. Shuffle back to cone B and touch it with your left hand.

7. Run backward as quickly as possible past cone A, the finish.

8. The test score is the best time of three trials.

For safety at the finish, a spotter should be positioned three meters behind cone A to catch players in case they fall while running backward. Players who cross one foot in front of the other, fail to touch the base of the cones, or fail to face forward throughout the test should be disqualified.

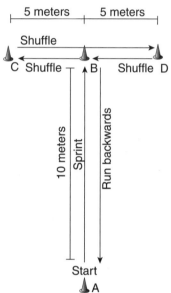

RUNNING CLOCK DRILL, ONE TIME

Purpose: To measure speed and agility. One Running Clock Drill is completed (see drill instructions on page 25). The test is appropriate for all positions and assesses multidirectional speed and agility.

Procedure

1. Follow steps 1 through 6 under Procedure on page 26.

2. The time taken to complete one lap of the Running Clock Drill course is recorded to the tenth of a second.

STRENGTH AND POWER TESTS

Three tests assess different aspects of strength and power.

1. Side Ramp measures the control and endurance of the core stabilizing muscles.

2. Three-Repetition Maximum evaluates maximum strength.

3. Vertical Jump tests explosive leg power.

The 10-meter sprint is also a good indicator of explosive power.

SIDE RAMP

Purpose: To measure the control and endurance of the lateral core stabilizing muscles.

Equipment and area: Stopwatch and flat mat (to support elbows).

Procedure

1. Position yourself in a full side bridge position on your right or left side with your legs straight. Extend your top foot in front of your lower foot for support. Lift your hip off the floor so that your elbow and feet support your body, creating a straight line from head to toe. Place your opposite hand on the supporting shoulder.

2. The length of time from when the Side Ramp position is reached until failure—that is, when your back is no longer straight and your hip is lowered—is recorded with the stopwatch.

3. Take five minutes for recovery before testing the other side.

4. Compare the performance on the two sides.

THREE-REPETITION MAXIMUM

Purpose: To measure maximum strength. This test identifies the maximum load (in kilograms) a player can lift for three repetitions, a variable known as the three-repetition maximum (3RM). Any loaded strength exercise can be used, such as a Back Squat, Front Squat, or Bench Press. It must be stressed that maximal lifting is hazardous and only experienced weight trainers should conduct testing of this type. Another strength testing option, particularly for the inexperienced weight trainer, is the Concept 2 Dyno. The Dyno offers three core exercises: Leg Press, Bench Press, and Bench Pull. Simply apply the 3RM protocol to these exercises.

Equipment and area: Stopwatch; free-weight equipment, including a barbell and a range of discs and collars; and two spotters.

Procedure

1. Attempt to lift the barbell to determine your 3RM by trial and error. After each attempt, increase or decrease the load by two and a half to five kilograms depending on the outcome of the attempt.

2. Take at least three minutes' rest between attempts.

VERTICAL JUMP TEST

Purpose: To measure explosive leg power. This test predicts acceleration and jumping performance. It is appropriate for all positions.

Equipment and area: Broom handle and infrared jump mat (or another type of electronic jump mat).

Procedure

1. Warm up thoroughly, and do at least three full-effort vertical jumps.

2. Position the broom handle across your shoulders behind your neck, holding it with your hands to prevent your arms from assisting you with the jump.

3. Perform three maximal vertical jumps, pausing for five seconds between each jump. First squat down to whatever depth you choose and then immediately explode upward for maximal height, landing with erect posture.

4. The height of each of three jumps is recorded in centimeters. The highest jump is the test score.

BODY MASS AND BODY FAT TESTS

Purpose: To measure the body mass and estimate the percentage of the mass that is fat (the fat mass). Body mass alone is a poor indicator of growth and body fat, because it does not distinguish between fat mass and fat-free mass. Periodic measuring of body mass and body fat will chart changes in body composition. The recommended way to measure fat mass is skinfold measurement.

Equipment and area: Weighing scale and a skinfold caliper.

Procedure

1. Players must be weighed at the same time of day and on the same day of the week to ensure that the measurements are reliable. Do not weigh after a training session unless you are comparing pre- and postexercise body mass to monitor fluid loss. The same tester should use the same scale and caliper each time.

2. Instruct the player to stand still on a calibrated scale in minimal clothing. Record the mass in kilograms.

3. Using a skinfold caliper, measure the thickness of specific skinfolds, applying a four- or seven-point body fat protocol. The sum of the skinfolds in millimeters is used to estimate body fat percentage. Find full guidelines for measuring skinfold thickness and prediction tables for estimating body fat in *Practical Body Composition* by Timothy Lohman (Human Kinetics 1995).

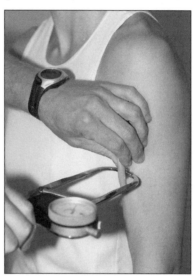

TEAM AVERAGE RESULTS FOR PROFESSIONAL MALE AND ELITE FEMALE RUGBY PLAYERS

The averages shown in tables 3.6 and 3.7 can be used to gauge individual and team levels of rugby-related conditioning. Note that acceleration tests start with a touch pad, which results in times that are slower than those that permit a one-meter flying start using a timing gate.

Table 3.6   Team Averages and Rankings for Professional Male Rugby Players

Test	Average	Good	Excellent
Ten-Meter Acceleration Test (touch-pad start)	2.10 to 2.25 s.	2.00 to 2.10 s.	<2.00 s.
Thirty-Meter Acceleration Test (touch-pad start)	4.25 to 4.45 s.	4.00 to 4.25 s.	<4.00 s.
Flying 30-Meter Speed Test	3.60 to 3.80 s.	3.40 to 3.60 s.	<3.40 s.
T Test	10.5 to 11.5 s.	9.5 to 10.5 s.	<9.5 s.
Running Clock Drill, One Time	24.0 to 25.5 s.	22.0 to 24.0 s.	<22 s.
Side Ramp	60 to 75 s.	75 to 90 s.	>90 s.
3RM Bench Press	110 to 120 kg	120 to 135 kg	>135 kg
3RM Power Clean	85 to 100 kg	100 to 115 kg	>115 kg
Vertical Jump Test (no arm assistance)	32 to 37 cm	37 to 45 cm	>45 cm
Body fat percentage	12.5 to 15%	10 to 12.5%	<10%

Table 3.7   Team Averages and Rankings for Elite Female Rugby Players

Test	Average	Good	Excellent
Ten-Meter Acceleration Test (touch-pad start)	2.50 to 2.75 s.	2.20 to 2.50 s.	<2.20 s.
Thirty-Meter Acceleration Test (touch-pad start)	4.75 to 5.25 s.	4.50 to 4.75 s.	<4.50 s.
Flying 30-Meter Speed Test	4.00 to 4.30 s.	3.70 to 4.00 s.	<3.70 s.
T Test	11.5 to 12.5 s.	10.5 to 11.5 s.	<10.5 s.
Running Clock Drill, One Time	26.0 to 28 s.	24.0 to 26.0 s.	<24 s.
Side Ramp	60 to 75 s.	75 to 90 s.	>90 s.
3RM Bench Press	55 to 65 kg	65 to 80 kg	>80 kg
3RM Power Clean	60 to 70 kg	70 to 80 kg	>80 kg
Vertical Jump Test (no arm assistance)	26 to 32 cm	32 to 39 cm	>39 cm
Body fat percentage	22 to 26%	18 to 22%	<18%

CHAPTER 4

WARM-UP DRILLS

The *warm-up* involves the activities that are performed at the beginning of a training session. Although warm-up drills do increase body temperature, they also increase the metabolic rate so that energy is released faster and muscles become more elastic, bridging the physiological divide between normal activity and high-intensity training.

Warm-up routines are versatile and should be altered to suit different workouts and the needs of the team or individual. They can be used to rehearse movements that will be the focus of the training session, such as passing, or to recruit muscles that will later be challenged to perform more demanding tasks, as with control drills done prior to explosive lifting.

The length of the warm-up depends on the content of the training session, but on average, a warm-up lasts 15 to 20 minutes. It should occupy about a quarter of your total training time to gain maximum benefits.

AIMS AND BENEFITS OF THE WARM-UP

The primary goals of the warm-up are to prepare for and reduce the potential for injury during the training session. Functional movement patterns that are specific to those in the body of the training session and recruit muscles that enhance the quality of those movements must be employed. Warming up provides these benefits:

- Increases body temperature to increase muscle elasticity and reduce joint friction
- Activates appropriate muscles and muscle groups
- Stimulates the cardiorespiratory and nervous systems
- Shortens reaction time
- Improves coordination
- Allows players to rehearse movement patterns
- Gets players mentally prepared for training

POWER-UP

The Power-Up is a warm-up session performed several hours before competition, most commonly by track athletes and cyclists. Rugby players and teams are starting to include the Power-Up in their prematch preparations, however.

Elite cyclist Lance Armstrong performs a 90-minute Power-Up cycling workout in the morning before an afternoon 49-kilometer time trial and then another 15-minute cycling session that includes several maximum bursts within 30 minutes of the trial. These two warm-ups prepare Armstrong's body for the main event by energizing his muscles and reminding his nervous system of the cycling movement pattern. The first session also helps him to recover from the previous day's racing. For rugby players, the Power-Up has the same benefits. It may include a short aerobic session (such as a 10-minute jog) or combine speed, agility, strength, and power drills to recruit and excite muscles without fatiguing them.

Dan's Top Tip

In the morning before a game, I often perform several minutes of foot-speed drills followed by stretches, balance and re-action drills, and light and fast explosive lifts like cleans and hang snatches. This helps me feel sharp and energized during the buildup to a game.

WARM-UP DRILLS

The warm-up routines that appear at the end of this chapter will improve your performance when you use them before rugby training, competition, and explosive lifting. These routines incorporate some of the warm-up drills in this section, divided into four categories:

- Partner drills
- Functional stretches
- Team drills
- Contact drills

PARTNER DRILLS

These drills can be used as a warm-up before most conditioning sessions.

PARTNER PASSING MEDLEY

Purpose: To focus on passing and catching skills and develop stability and movement strength.

Equipment and area: One rugby ball per pair of players.

a

Procedure: The Partner Passing Medley involves a series of eight different passing drills and positions. Partners line up three to five meters apart, depending on skill level. Each drill includes 20 passes (10 per player).

1. Stand sidelong to a partner. The players alternate between a standard spin pass off the left hand and then the right, with feet shoulder-width apart, not staggered. Aim to keep your feet stationary and finish with your hands pointing where you want the ball to go (outstretched and on top of the ball). Rotate 180 degrees between each pass.

2. Repeat step 1, but both players stand on one leg.

3. Each player lobs a pass to the partner, who jumps to catch the ball (figure a).

4. Each player rolls a pass to the partner, who bends down to receive the ball.

5. At a distance of two meters, both players stand on their toes and pass the ball using both hands back and forth above their heads.

6. Partners face each other and pass the ball back and forth (standard pass, not a spin pass). On receiving the ball, each player twists and performs a dummy pass first to the left and behind, then to the right and behind, and then passes the ball back to the partner.

7. With both players on their knees like goalkeepers, they pass the ball back and forth, trying to catch the ball to encourage controlled contact with the ground (figure b).

8. Each player makes an overhead pass (lineout throw), using both hands to control the ball.

Progression: Lengthen the distance between partners based on their skill level.

b

FUNCTIONAL STRETCHES

Functional stretching lubricates the joints through rhythmic movements and gradually increases the range of motion by warming the muscles. A joint is taken through its full range of motion in movements generated by the muscles and the momentum of the body.

HURDLE STRETCH

Purpose: To stretch the trunk and hip muscles by using hurdles or a partner. This stretch prepares you for deep squatting and flexed movements like tackling, mauling, and scrummaging.

Equipment and area: Track hurdle (optional).

Procedure

1. Set a track hurdle at maximum height. If no hurdle is available, two players face each other and link their hands for support. The pair assumes a semisquatting position to create a space for you—the stretching player—to move under.

2. Crouch sideways in front of the hurdle or pair of players and move laterally beneath it and then back to the start position.

Make this movement 12 times, with five seconds' rest between repetitions. You can also perform this drill when you face the hurdle or have your back to it.

Key point: Allow your spine to flex to pass under the hurdle. The movement should be slow and controlled.

Progression: Gradually reduce the hurdle height.

LUNGE AND REACH

Purpose: To focus on the hip flexors, trunk flexion, and rotation. This stretch prepares you for such movements as reaching to catch a ball or make a tackle.

Procedure

1. Perform a forward lunge.

2. At the end of the lunge range, reach forward with both of your hands to touch the floor to the outside of the lead leg and hold the position for three seconds.

3. Return to the start position and repeat the movement, lunging to the other side. Make eight lunges with each leg, gradually increasing the reach.

Key points

- Perform the drill slowly and with control.

- Allow your trunk to flex.

- Hollow and brace your abdominal muscles to support your lower back. Refer to the core stability guidelines on page 78 for advice on performing an Abdominal Hollow and Brace.

KNEE AND HEEL RAISE

Purpose: To stretch the calves and hip extensors. This prepares you for accelerating and running at high speeds.

Procedure

1. Perform a high knee raise with one leg while rising onto the toes of the support foot and pushing both of your hands above your head.

2. Hold this position for a few seconds and then return to the start position. Do 10 repetitions for each leg.

Key point: Hollow and brace the abdominal muscles to support your lower back.

Progression: Hold a rugby ball and change the arm movement to a diagonal reach above your head.

ARM SWINGS

Purpose: To stretch the shoulder muscles. This stretch prepares the shoulders for reaching to catch the ball and make various contact movements.

Procedure

1. Stand with your feet shoulder-width apart and your knees slightly flexed, with your arms hanging naturally at your sides.

2. Swinging your arms forward and upward and then continuing backward and downward, create a large circle with each straight arm. The movement should be controlled and rhythmic, and the aim is to reach as high as possible. Perform 10 forward swings and then change the direction of the swing to backward and upward for 10 more swings. Do three sets, with 15 seconds' rest between them.

Key point: Maintain a neutral neck—do not look up or down.

Progression: Move one arm forward and upward while the other arm moves backward and upward, allowing your trunk to sway from side to side.

LEG SWINGS

Purpose: To stretch the hamstrings, adductors, and abductors. This prepares the legs and hips for high-speed running and changing direction.

Procedure

1. While standing with the support of a partner, post, or wall, swing one leg straight out in front of you, focusing on controlling the movement with your abdominal muscles. As your leg swings back to the ground, scuff your foot along its surface. Gradually increase the range of each movement by swinging—not thrusting—your leg upward.

2. Perform two sets of 10 repetitions with each leg. Then repeat the drill, but swing your leg out to the side and then across your body.

Key points

- Hollow and brace your abdominal muscles to support your lower back during the leg swing.

- Do not swing your leg too far away from or across your body.

TEAM DRILLS

Passing grids are ideal warm-up drills before training sessions or competitive rugby. They involve groups of players performing multi-directional running, passing, and catching skills while communicating and working as a team. The intensity of the drill can range from jogging to the maximum running pace, and only a small area is required.

CENTER CONE GRID

Purpose: To warm up a group of players by using multidirectional running, passing, and catching skills; communication; and teamwork.

Equipment and area: Five cones, four rugby balls, and an area of 8 to 15 square meters, depending on ground conditions.

Procedure

1. Create a square grid with five cones, placing one in the middle of the grid. Cones should be placed between 8 (on heavy ground in poor weather) and 15 meters apart (on firm ground in good weather). Divide the players into four groups and place a ball on each corner cone.

2. The first player in each group jogs to the center cone, carrying the ball in both hands. The player then steps left toward the next group of players and passes the ball to the player waiting at that cone. That player repeats the drill.

3. After players pass the ball, they join the line at the cone they passed to.

Coaching commands and options: The coach dictates the type of pass and running direction of the players with periodic commands.

- "Change direction!" Players break to the right from the center cone instead of to the left.

- "My down, my up!" Instead of passing from the center cone, players place the ball on the ground a yard in front of the player waiting at the next cone, who picks up the ball and repeats the drill.

- "Jump catch!" Players lob the ball so the player at the cone must jump to catch it.

- "Gut pass!" The player to receive the ball meets the player carrying it between the center and grid cones. The ball carrier places the ball in the midriff section of the crouching, oncoming player.

- "Pop pass!" The player to receive the ball meets the ball carrier midway between the grid and center cones, where the ball carrier executes a pop pass.

Key points

- Change the running direction or type of pass every 15 to 20 seconds.

- Encourage players to crouch low when turning and when receiving the gut pass.

- Encourage the players to communicate.

- Ensure that players always go to the center cone before moving toward the next cone.

- Begin this drill at a jogging pace and gradually increase the exertion to three-quarters pace.

Progression: Have players do an exercise—for example, three push-ups—while they wait in line for their turn.

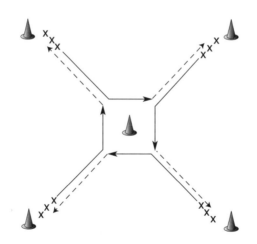

UNION JACK

Purpose: To warm up a group of players by using multidirectional running, passing, and catching skills; communication; and teamwork.

Equipment and area: Eight cones, two rugby balls, and an area of 6 to 10 square meters.

Procedure

1. Create a square grid with eight cones placed an equal distance apart (between three and five meters). Split the players into eight equal groups—one for each cone—and give one ball to each of two groups in opposite corners.

2. The players with the balls pass them to the players on their left. The receiving players repeat the drill.

3. The passing players follow their passes to join the end of the line at the cone they passed to.

4. Once all players have made several passes and runs to their left, the drill continues but the pass and run is to the right.

5. Once all players have made several passes and runs to their right, the drill continues with a pass to the left but followed by a run across the grid to the opposite cone. Corner cone players run diagonally across the inside of the grid to the opposite corner cone, and join the end of the line at that cone, while players at other cones simply run to the opposite cone (straight across the grid) and join the end of the line at that cone. This sequence is repeated around the grid for several passes per player before passing in the opposite direction.

Coaching commands and options: The coach dictates the type of pass and the running direction of the players with periodic commands. The coach may also introduce an extra ball.

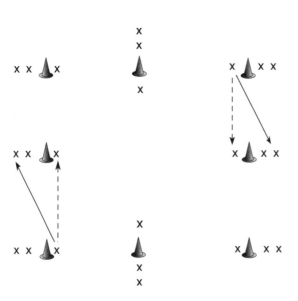

- "Change direction!" Players pass to their right instead of their left and either follow the pass or go to the opposite or diagonal cone.

- "Go forward two cones!" Players follow their passes but join the end of the line at the cone beyond the cone they passed to. This increases the intensity of the drill as players have to run farther.

- "Jump catch!" Players lob the ball so the player at the cone must jump to catch it.
- "Roll pass!" Players roll the ball to the next player.

Key points

- Change the running direction or type of pass every 15 to 20 seconds.
- Encourage the players to communicate.
- Begin this drill at a jogging pace and gradually increase the exertion to three-quarters pace.

COMPASS DRILL

Purpose: To warm up a group of players by using multidirectional running, communication, and teamwork. The players try to maintain a defensive line while obeying coaching commands.

Procedure

1. The players stand in a line an arm's-length apart from each other and face the coach, who stands facing them from 10 to 15 meters away.
2. By pointing, the coach signals to the players to move in a particular direction—lateral left, lateral right, backward, forward, or down and back up when pointing both arms at the ground. The players must react to the coach's command and maintain a flat defensive line while performing the movements.

Key points

- The defensive line should remain flat while the players change direction in response to the coach's arm commands.
- Players should stay an arm's-length away from each other.
- Encourage a high level of communication and have the players call out the direction in which the coach asks them to move, for example, by shouting, "Left, left, left!"

```
X
X
X |——— 10-15 meters ———| Coach
X
X
```

CONTACT DRILLS

Contact drills are used toward the end of a warm-up routine as part of the progression to full-body contact drills or high-intensity pad drills.

GET UP! STAY DOWN!

Purpose: To challenge players' ability to push up from the floor against resistance. This drill prepares players for dynamic movements such as getting up quickly after hitting the ground.

Procedure

1. Lie facedown on the floor as your partner stands over you.

2. Try for 10 seconds to get up from the floor while your partner tries to prevent this. After 10 seconds' rest, change roles and repeat until each player has tried to get up four times.

Key points

- If a player succeeds in getting up within 10 seconds, that player repeats the drill until he or she is unsuccessful. Count the number of successful "ups."

- The partner who is trying to keep the other down must stay on his or her feet. No lying down on the player who is trying to get up!

STEP-UP PAD DRILL

Purpose: To warm up and improve reaction times in large groups of players by using multidirectional running, communication, and teamwork in a defensive contact pad drill.

Equipment and area: Four cones, five contact pad holders, and a rugby ball.

Procedure

1. Position three groups (D1, D2, and D3) of five players each along the try line, with one meter between each player and two cones separating the groups. Across from the middle group, approximately three meters away, position five contact pad holders, with a cone on each side of them. Place a ball on the floor adjacent to the contact pad holders.

2. The aim of the drill is for the groups to react to the ball and step up as a defensive line. When the coach picks up the ball, as a player would when a ball is released from a ruck, the groups sprint to the cones and contact pad holders. The middle group (D2) tackles the pads while the other groups go to the tackle line.

3. The groups immediately return to the try line, rotating their positions along the way. Group D1 backpedals laterally to the center position, D3 runs all the way across to replace D1, and D2 backpedals laterally to the position originally held by D3. This constitutes one repetition.

4. The coach then picks up the ball and repeats the drill until all the players have made at least two tackles on the pads. Then, make other players be the pad holders and repeat the drill for the third time.

D1 D1 D1 D1 D1 🔺 D2 D2 D2 D2 D2 🔺 D3 D3 D3 D3 D3

Coach

X X X X X

Contact pad holders

Key points

- Encourage the players to call "out" or "up" when the coach picks up the ball to signify ball release.
- Players should face forward at all times to keep the attackers (pad holders) in view.
- The amount of resistance the contact pad holders put up against the tacklers should prevent too much backward movement of the pad holders (two meters maximum).

Progression: Increase the demands of the drill by instructing the players to lie chest-down on the floor at the start.

SAMPLE WARM-UP ROUTINES

Explosive Lifting Warm-Up

1. Eight minutes of cycling or rowing.

2. Two minutes of active stretching.

3. Control drill set: (a) Bent Knee to Sky, 10 times each leg; (b) Squat and Squeeze, 5-second hold, 2 times; (c) T Raises, 10 times. Repeat for 3 sets.

4. Two 20-second bursts on a cycle or rowing machine, with 20 seconds' recovery between bursts.

5. Two minutes of active stretches.

6. Core stabilization drill set: (a) Arm and Leg Raise, 10 times; (b) Single-Leg Bridge, 5 times with each leg. Repeat the set.

7. Focusing on technique, perform at least 2 warm-up sets of each lift (for example, the Power Pull). For example, do 4 repetitions at 40 percent of 1RM and 4 repetitions at 60 percent of 1RM.

See chapter 6 for control and core stabilization drills.

Speed and Agility Training Warm-Up

1. Partner Passing Medley, repeat for 2 sets of 12 passes.

2. Two minutes of active stretching.

3. Top-Five Ladder Drills: (a) Drill 1, one foot in each square. On leaving the ladder, jog backward to the start and repeat Drill 1 for 3 repetitions; (b) Drill 2, both feet in each square. On leaving the ladder, shuffle sideways back to the start, alternating left and right side lead legs, and repeat Drill 2 for 3 repetitions. Allow 1 minute of rest between (a) and (b).

4. Two minutes of active stretching.

5. Core stabilization and movement strength drills: (a) Leg Raise and Support, 15 times with each leg; (b) Rotating Ramp, 3 times with 15 seconds' rest between sets; (c) Lunge and Reach, 6 repetitions with each leg; (d) Backward Lunge, 6 repetitions with each leg.

The Partner Passing Medley is described earlier in this chapter. See chapter 6 for control and core stabilization drills and chapter 7 for the Top-Five Ladder Drills.

Prematch Warm-Up

The prematch warm-up is similar to a rugby training warm-up, but it generally lasts longer and takes the same form every time. The routine should be rehearsed during training sessions to ensure that it will run smoothly and on schedule. A prematch warm-up may include several distinct elements, including passing drills, contact drills, functional stretching, and a brief tactical drill such as lineout practice or semi-opposed team drills. Individual players' positional drills should be performed prior to the team warm-up.

The following routine takes approximately 20 minutes and should be completed within 8 to 10 minutes of kickoff.

Stage 1 (10 minutes)

Individual preparation. Players practice position-specific drills with balls. For example, the scrum-half can perform specific passing drills, hookers can work on lineout throws, and designated kickers can do low-intensity kicking drills. Players may also perform control drills, foot-speed drills, or passing drills in pairs.

Stage 2 (8 minutes)

Union Jack (run to opposite cone) for 60 seconds, 10 seconds' rest, then repeat in the opposite direction.

Movement stretches and fluid intake (2 minutes).

Center Cone Grid for 90 seconds (vary the type of pass).

Movement stretches (2 minutes).

Stage 3 (3 minutes)

Separate players into forwards and backs for 3 minutes; forwards practice lineout plays, backs practice back-line passing and moves.

Stage 4 (1 minute)

Movement stretches and fluid intake.

Stage 5 (1 minute)

Step-Up Pad Drill (2 hits per group).

CHAPTER 5

FLEXIBILITY AND POSTURE DRILLS

The quest for improved athletic performance and injury prevention is incomplete without incorporating a dedicated approach to flexibility and posture training. Failing to appreciate the importance of these qualities can undo all of the benefits achieved with other types of conditioning and increase the chance of injury while reducing movement efficiency and effectiveness.

This chapter covers four methods of flexibility development: static, active, self-release, and functional stretching drills. These interactive methods of flexibility training use foam rollers, Swiss balls, and towels as tools. Players should include all four methods in their flexibility and posture program. The principles of posture management and ways to optimize your posture are also discussed.

FLEXIBILITY

Flexibility refers to the length of a muscle and the range of motion about a joint. Poor flexibility negatively affects several aspects of rugby performance and can lead to injury. The most common problems in players—tight hamstrings and buttocks, short hip flexors, and rigid shoulders—manifest themselves in several ways:

- Reduced stride length
- Poor posture
- Muscle imbalances
- Impaired ability to reach for tackles and passes
- Reduced movement efficiency (fighting the resistance caused by tight and short muscles and immobile joints requires more energy)

Flexibility drills improve your rugby performance by allowing you to sprint faster and change direction effectively and efficiently. The dynamic and unexpected movements performed in rugby are also less risky when flexibility is sound.

POSTURE

Ideal posture allows the joints and muscles to perform at their best. Defined as the structural alignment of the body, posture considers the positioning of key areas of the body, including the neck, shoulder blades, and pelvis. Figure 5.1 contrasts poor, lordotic posture, with excessive arching of the lower back and slouching, and ideal posture. Lordotic posture, which is associated with weak core muscles and tight hip flexors, is usually the result of overemphasizing such drills as the Bench Press and neglecting core stabilization and pulling strength drills.

Poor posture is at the root of many preventable sports injuries, and it has been shown that more energy is required to move the body when postural alignment is poor. Lower-back pain, which reduces the ability to train and perform effectively, is a common symptom among players with poor posture. Drills for improving posture appear at the end of this chapter.

FLEXIBILITY DRILLS

Follow these guidelines when performing the flexibility drills:

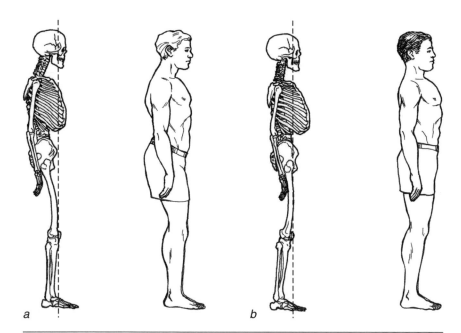

Figure 5.1   Compare (a) poor posture with (b) ideal posture.

- Breathe deeply and do not hold your breath.
- Stretch to a point of moderate tension so that you feel mild discomfort but no pain. (Pain is a result of the muscle trying to shorten.)
- Spend extra time working on muscles that are chronically tight.
- Focus your mind on the muscles being stretched and encourage them to relax.
- Do not stretch until you have increased your body temperature through exercise.
- Compare the range of motion you achieve in your left and right arms and legs during flexibility drills. If there is a noticeable difference, consult a physiotherapist to diagnose the cause and remedy it.

Dan's Top Tip

Do your flexibility routines in a warm room while you listen to relaxing music. It is also a good idea to have your flexibility and posture assessed by a qualified professional who can help you individualize your flexibility and posture program.

STATIC STRETCHING DRILLS

Static stretching, a traditional approach to flexibility, involves passively taking a muscle to a point of tension and holding the stretch for a minimum of 20 seconds.

CALF STRETCH

Purpose: To statically stretch the upper- and lower-calf musculature.

Procedure

1. To stretch the upper calf, lean against a partner, post, or wall with your right leg straightened so that it is two or three feet behind the left leg, which is flexed.

2. With both feet pointing toward the support, slowly push the heel of the right foot into the ground and the hips forward to intensify the stretch, then hold for a minimum of 20 seconds and repeat with the opposite leg.

a

3. To stretch the lower calf, assume the same position as for step 1, but also flex the right leg and move the right foot closer to the heel of the left leg.

4. Allow the right leg to progressively take on more body weight to intensify the stretch and hold for a minimum of 20 seconds, then repeat with the opposite leg.

b

HIP FLEXOR STRETCH

Purpose: To statically stretch the hip flexors. Tight hip flexors are often associated with poor posture.

Procedure

1. Slowly move into a lunge position, resting the top of your rear foot's instep on the floor. Move the rear hip forward and downward until tension is felt in the hip flexors.

2. Raise up and over your head the arm on the same side as the leg being stretched to intensify the stretch while placing the opposite arm on the lead leg for support.

3. Squeeze the buttock of the rear leg to intensify the stretch, hollow the lower abdominal muscles for lower-back support, and hold for a minimum of 20 seconds, then repeat with the opposite leg.

TOWEL HAMSTRING STRETCH

Purpose: To statically stretch the hamstrings. Using the towel helps to intensify the stretch and maintain neutral neck and lower-back positions.

Procedure

1. Lying on the floor, wrap a towel around the instep of one foot and, keeping your pelvis on the floor and your leg extended, slowly pull the leg toward your face.

2. Hold for a minimum of 20 seconds, flex the leg, slowly return the leg to the floor, and repeat with the opposite leg.

3. Repeat the drill with the leg slightly bent (10 to 15 degrees) to focus the stretch on the "belly" of the hamstring.

ACTIVE STRETCHING DRILLS

Active stretching is the process of moving a joint into a range of motion by using agonists and synergists. For example, raising one straight leg to the front while standing uses the quads and hip flexors to stretch the hamstrings. The tension in the thigh and hip flexor muscles helps to relax the hamstring, thus improving the range of motion. Players should hold these stretches for a minimum of 10 to 20 seconds.

SWISS BALL SWAY AND REACH

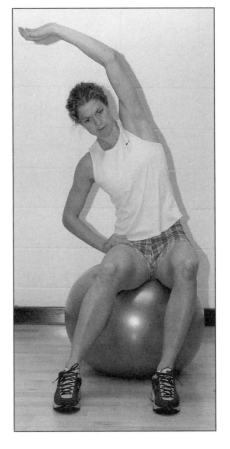

Purpose: To actively stretch the psoas and back muscles. Using a Swiss ball helps to intensify the stretch by allowing a lateral movement (sway) in one direction and an opposite movement (reach) in the other direction.

Procedure

1. Sit in a neutral position on a Swiss ball, meaning that you draw your body upward by lifting with the muscles at the back of the head, lengthening the spine.

2. Reach up with your right arm until it is over your head and slowly sway your hips to the right while leaning and reaching to the left with your right arm. The stretch is felt between the hip and the shoulder and can be intensified by swaying and reaching farther.

3. Hold the stretch for a minimum of 10 seconds, then repeat on the opposite side.

GROIN STRETCH

Purpose: To actively stretch the groin muscles.

Procedure

1. While standing, step your left leg to a position 45 degrees in front of your body, keeping your left leg straight and supporting the majority of your body weight on your flexed right leg. You are focusing the stretch on the inside of your left leg.

2. Push the foot of the left leg into the floor and apply pressure to the left hip with your left hand to intensify the stretch.

3. Hold the stretch for 10 to 20 seconds and then repeat it with the opposite leg.

TOWEL CHEST AND SHOULDER STRETCH

Purpose: To actively stretch the chest and shoulder muscles. The towel creates tension that intensifies the stretch. This stretch also improves shoulder and neck posture by lengthening tight chest muscles and the external rotators of the shoulder.

Procedure

1. Stand with your feet spread and hold a long towel or stick with your hands at opposite ends. With both hands, slowly raise the towel or stick above and then behind your head until your arms,

behind you, are parallel with the floor. Maintain neutral body alignment at all times and do not arch your lower back to facilitate the stretch.

2. Hold for five seconds, then return to the start position and repeat for up to 15 stretches.

Key point: Monitor your progress by measuring the width of your grip: the narrower your grip, the better your chest and shoulder flexibility.

a

b

SELF-RELEASE STRETCHING DRILLS

Self-release stretching is a form of self-massage that reduces tissue tightness and helps to increase flexibility. This approach involves finding "tight spots" with a foam roller and holding that position until the muscle softens. Rolling the foam roller back and forth over the tight spot also releases it.

Perform self-release drills before other flexibility drills to maximize the benefits of your flexibility routine.

ILIOTIBIAL BAND SELF-RELEASE

Purpose: To self-release and stretch the iliotibial (IT) band.

Procedure

1. While lying on your side, position the roller at the rugby-shorts line (midway between the hip and knee) on the outer side of the leg, between your leg and the floor. Roll it slowly up and down the thigh until you feel a tight spot in the muscle, then hold for 60 seconds.

2. Use the opposite leg to control the amount of pressure being applied. For full pressure, place the opposite leg on top of the leg being stretched.

3. Repeat this procedure at all of the tight spots along the IT band, but do not use the foam roller on the knee joint.

GLUTEAL SELF-RELEASE

Purpose: To self-release and stretch the gluteus muscles.

Procedure

1. While sitting on a mat, position the roller directly beneath the right gluteal muscle, placing your left leg either behind your right leg to focus more on the back side of the gluteal muscle or in front of your right leg to focus more on the front side of the muscle.

2. Hold the roller on tight spots for 60 seconds or move it back and forth through a small range (two to three inches) until you experience release.

3. Repeat this procedure until all tight spots are gone, then repeat the drill with the opposite leg.

CALF SELF-RELEASE

Purpose: To self-release and stretch the calves.

Procedure

1. While sitting on the floor with your legs extended, position the roller under your legs, midway between your knees and ankles, and support your body's weight with your hands and calves only.

2. Roll the foam roll up and down the calf muscles' bellies or hold it on tight spots for 60 seconds. Intensify the stretch by crossing one leg over the other and placing all of your weight on one calf.

BACK SELF-RELEASE

Purpose: To self-release and stretch the mid- and upper-back muscles. Thoracic spine release may also occur during this stretch and will be heard or felt as "clunks."

Procedure

1. Lying on the floor, position the roller directly beneath your midback (bra-strap level) and distribute your body weight among your feet, the gluteal muscles, and the foam roller.

2. Shift more of your body weight to the foam roller and slowly extend your arms behind your head, holding the roller on tight spots for 60 seconds.

FUNCTIONAL STRETCHING DRILLS

Functional stretches use the movement generated by muscles and the momentum of the body to take a joint through the full available range of motion. They incorporate multiplanar movements, with the muscles controlling the speed, intensity, and direction of the stretch.

These drills, which are ideal as part of a warm-up before most training sessions and are covered in detail on pages 42 to 45 in chapter 4, Warm-Up Drills, include the following:

- Hurdle Stretch
- Lunge and Reach
- Knee and Heel Raise
- Arm Swings
- Leg Swings

FLEXIBILITY ROUTINE

To improve flexibility, the best approach is to combine the four methods of stretching in an integrated routine.

Integrated Flexibility Routine (40 minutes)

Stage 1: Warm-Up (8-12 minutes)

To increase your body temperature, cycle, row, or jog for 8 to 12 minutes in warm clothing.

Stage 2: Self-Release Drills (10 minutes)

Back Self-Release (3 minutes)

Iliotibial Band Self-Release (3 minutes)

Gluteal Self-Release (3 minutes)

Stage 3: Static Stretch Drills (10 minutes)

Hip Flexor Stretch—Do three sets of 30 seconds with each leg

Towel Hamstring Stretch—Do three sets of 30 seconds with each leg

Stage 4: Active Stretching Drills (5 minutes)

Swiss Ball Sway and Reach—Do six sets of 5 seconds on each side

Towel Chest and Shoulder Stretch—Do three sets of 10 five-second stretches with 60 seconds' rest between sets

Stage 5: Functional Stretching Drills (5 minutes)

Lunge and Reach—Do five repetitions with each leg

Hurdle Stretch—Do three sets of five repetitions with lateral movement and two sets of five repetitions with forward movement.

Stage 5 drills are detailed in chapter 4, Warm-Up Drills.

POSTURE DRILLS

The following are not workout drills, but rather "habit" drills that you should perform several times a day. With consistent practice and awareness, your body will learn to automatically assume correct posture.

FINDING NEUTRAL

Purpose: To learn and rehearse *neutral alignment*. This term is used to describe correct posture.

Procedure: To find the neutral position, stand relaxed and then draw yourself upward using the muscles at the back of your head to lengthen your spine. Your shoulder blades should be relaxed and down away from your ears, your pelvis should be level under your shoulders, and your stomach should be slightly flattened.

STANDING POSTURE

Purpose: To develop correct standing posture.

Procedure

1. While standing relaxed, pull in your abdomen to hollow it and squeeze your buttocks (30 percent effort).
2. Lift your chest and gently pull your shoulders back and down.

3. Lengthen your spine while keeping your chin tucked in. Imagining that a helium balloon is attached to the crown of your head may be helpful. Breathe normally.

4. Hold this position for 10 to 20 seconds, rest for 10 seconds, and repeat. Do several sets throughout the day.

SITTING POSTURE

Purpose: To develop correct sitting posture. Although you should in general follow the principles set out here, it is important to move regularly and to vary your sitting posture. Prolonged sitting in any position is hard on the lumbar spine and surrounding muscles.

Procedure

1. Lengthen your spine while keeping your chin tucked in. Again, imagine that a helium balloon is attached to the crown of your head to keep yourself from slouching.

2. Sit tall with your shoulders back.

3. Subtly (10 percent effort) hollow your abdominal muscles and squeeze your buttocks slightly (10 percent effort).

4. Ensure that your feet are flat on the ground at slightly more than shoulder-width apart.

5. After several minutes in this position, change your posture by slouching slightly. After a few minutes, return to the original position.

PELVIC TILT

Purpose: To develop and learn a neutral hip/spine position. This means feeling and knowing where the hips are in relation to the spine. Controlling this movement is key to ensuring lower back safety during exercises including squatting, explosive lifting, and core stabilization drills.

Procedure

1. Lie on the floor with knees bent and feet flat on the floor. Position your hands on the front of your hips.

2. Rotate the pelvis backward and push your lower back into the floor by hollowing your abdominal muscles and squeezing your buttocks. Hold for three seconds. This is a backward tilt of the pelvis.

3. Rotate your hips in the opposite direction by tightening your lower back muscles so your lower back arches off the floor. Hold for three seconds. This is a forward tilt of the pelvis.

4. Repeat the forward and backward tilts for several repetitions. If you experience pain with backward or forward pelvic tilting stop performing the drill and consult a physiotherapist or physician.

5. To find your neutral position, stop at the midpoint between the backward and forward tilting motion. Hold this position, which should feel comfortable and natural, for five seconds. This is your strongest and safest hip/spine position and the position to be in when performing static and dynamic core stabilization drills and loaded strength and explosive lifting drills, which are covered in detail in chapter 6, Strength and Power Drills. This is also your optimal position when lifting in a lineout or pushing in a scrum.

POSTURE-ENHANCING STRENGTH DRILLS

All of the control and core stabilization drills in chapter 6, Strength and Power Drills, directly and positively influence posture by activating the stabilizing muscles of the neck, shoulder blades, and pelvis. Use them on a regular basis to ensure that you maintain correct posture.

STRENGTH AND POWER DRILLS

Strength and power development are the cornerstones of a successful rugby conditioning program; making or breaking a tackle, accelerating, and scrummaging are just a few of the situations in which a rugby player needs strength and power. Strength, which is a precursor to power, is defined as the ability to exert and withstand force. Strength drills are probably the most important component of conditioning, and they have many applications and can provide several benefits:

- Improved full-body control and stability
- Enhanced movement-pattern performance, such as mauling a ball better, tackling more effectively, and lifting or jumping higher in a lineout
- Enhanced fuel mix conditioning
- Improved acceleration

- Stronger basis for power development (also known as speed strength)
- Greater protection against injury by, for example, providing vital stability to joints and muscles

Several types of strength and power drills are used in progression. Figure 6.1 illustrates as a pyramid the path of progression that must be followed in strength and power training.

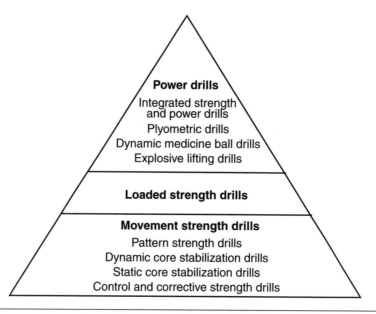

Figure 6.1 Pyramid of strength and power training drills.

MOVEMENT STRENGTH DRILLS

Movement strength drills develop a fundamental strength base and enhance the quality of movements by focusing on muscular control, stability, and strength. They are designed to reduce susceptibility to injury and improve the ability to perform such skills as reaching to catch a ball, twisting to off-load in contact, and making tackles. These drills are also precursors to loaded strength and power drills.

- **Control and corrective strength drills.** These drills activate specific muscles that stabilize the joints. These key muscles support the knee, hip, and shoulder joints during body contact and high-speed multidirectional running and reduce the chances of injury while encouraging efficient movement patterns.

• **Static and dynamic core stabilization drills.** These drills develop the trunk stability needed for a dynamic game like rugby. They encourage the key stabilizers of the trunk, including the abdominal, gluteal, lower– back, shoulder, and neck muscles, to support the efforts of the arms and legs. The following are benefits of core stabilization training: improved posture, more efficient use of muscle power, decreased risk of injury, increased stability in body contact and thus improved technique, and greater speed and agility.

These drills, which progress from static holds to dynamic movements, often involve using an unstable surface such as a Swiss ball or wobble board to stimulate and challenge the key stabilizing muscles. See figure 6.2 for some of the muscles worked in these drills.

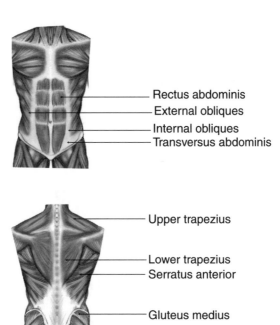

• **Pattern strength drills.** Pattern strength drills develop functional strength with motion and simulate many of the movements of rugby, such as lunging, twisting, and squatting. These body-weight drills include rotational and diagonal patterns in addition to flexion and extension. When supported by control strength and core stability, these drills ensure that the body works effectively as a linked system.

Figure 6.2 Muscles worked in the core stabilization drills.

LOADED STRENGTH DRILLS

With the progression from movement strength training to loaded strength drills, traditional resistance exercises are added to the program. These drills demand significant loading of large muscle groups and develop general and maximum strength. In combination with qualities developed in movement strength training, loaded strength training increases the rugby player's functional strength. The strength gained from loaded drills also permits the player to progress to power drills.

POWER DRILLS

Explosive movements are the highlight of rugby performance. Bursting past a defender and accelerating to make a big tackle require the fast application of strength. The power to perform these activities is developed by performing strength drills quickly—that's why it's called *speed strength.*

Power drills include explosive lifts like the Power Clean, plyometric jumping and bounding drills, and medicine ball drills. All of these drills use a load as resistance and should be performed explosively with control. Players must resist the temptation to progress to power drills until they have gone through several months of movement strength and loaded strength training.

TRAINING SYSTEMS AND TECHNIQUE

Various training systems are used for developing strength and power, allowing players and coaches to manipulate the application of drills. The most common systems are described in table 6.1. Approaches to training, including bodybuilding, rehabilitation, and technique are also reviewed.

Single- and multiple-set systems are more appropriately used during the initial stages of training, whereas pyramid and complex-training systems are suitable for a more experienced and conditioned player. The superset system is also excellent for developing elements of strength and power. For example, during a loaded strength phase of training, those drills may be paired with stability or pattern drills in, for example, a Back Squat superset with the Lunge and Dummy Pass drill.

Bodybuilding

Becoming stable, strong, and powerful does not necessarily mean getting bigger. Although there is a positive relationship between strength and size, the typical bodybuilding approach to strength training is

Table 6.1 Training Systems

System	Description
Single set	The player performs one set of each exercise. For example, 8 to 12 repetitions of each drill in a series of core stabilization drills may be performed.
Multiple set	The most popular system for pattern strength, loaded strength, and explosive lifting drills, it incorporates two or three warm-up sets of increasing resistance in the same drill before progressing to several sets at the same resistance.
Pyramid	This system can be approached from either direction, that is, from a light to a heavy load or from a heavy to a light load. A light load could be lifted for 8 to 12 repetitions during the first set, but in subsequent sets heavier loads and fewer repetitions are used, usually finishing with 1 or 2 repetitions at the heaviest load. A heavy-to-light pyramid starts with 1 or 2 repetitions at a high resistance and continues with lighter loads and more repetitions.
Superset	Incorporating versatility into strength and power training, this system uses sets of two or more different exercises—such as a pulling movement (as in the Bent-Over Row) immediately followed by a pushing movement (as in the Weighted Push-Up). Or, a core stabilization or pattern strength drill might be paired with a loaded strength drill.
Split routine	This very popular hypertrophy method of training involves performing different drills for the same body part and splitting routines. For example, on day 1, work might be done on the back, biceps, and legs, and on day 3, on the chest, shoulders, and triceps. This approach is suitable only during a hypertrophy phase of training.
Complex training	With this advanced system, the player uses heavy and light loads in the same set. The theory behind this is that once a heavy load has been lifted, there are high levels of muscle recruitment and nervous system excitement, which enhance performance during the lighter load set. For example, a 3RM Back Squat would be followed by 3 repetitions of a body-weight vertical jump.

inappropriate for rugby players. Players and coaches should follow the pyramid of strength and power training drills (see page 72) when designing their strength and power program. If increases in muscular size are deemed vital, they can be achieved by performing a high volume of pattern and loaded strength drills.

Technique

The most important principle in strength and power training is to use correct technique. Technique should never be sacrificed for the sake of the level of resistance, experimentation, or speed of movement. All strength and power exercises should be treated like skills—similar to kicking or passing—to be learned and taught in a way that will ensure effectiveness and prevent injury. In addition to following the guidelines that accompany all strength and power drills, players should also seek the advice of qualified weightlifting or strength and conditioning coaches.

Rehabilitation Strength Training

When a muscle is injured or subjected to prolonged inactivity, it first loses size and strength. This process reverses the levels of strength gained prior to the injury, but once the pain and swelling have subsided, movement and a program of low-level strength drills should be quickly started. For example, control and corrective strength drills are commonly used during rehabilitation from lower-back, knee, and shoulder injuries. These drills can be used for rehabilitation after injury:

- Control and corrective strength drills to encourage damaged muscles to regain muscle tone and nervous system firing
- Limited-range pattern strength drills to reintroduce movement strength with, for example, a limited-range lunge or miniature single-leg squats for knee-joint rehabilitation
- Static core stabilization drills in a progressive program to promote recovery from lower-back pain

Note that the drills and programs to be used in rehabilitation after serious injuries must be selected and supervised by a doctor or physiotherapist. Ultimately, the exercises chosen must be functional to return the player to competition. Ideally, muscle strength and performance should be at preinjury levels before the player is reintroduced to competition.

MOVEMENT STRENGTH DRILLS

CONTROL AND CORRECTIVE STRENGTH DRILLS

Using the appropriate muscles for certain movements is imperative for improving the quality of that movement, which in turn leads to increased power output and injury prevention.

Control drills help the muscles to activate, much like a command system. They may also be called corrective strength training drills in a rehabilitation setting, in reference to their goal of correcting the condition of muscles that have "switched off" as a result of damage or inactivity. Control drills should also be part of the warm-up before all training sessions, particularly those that concentrate on strength and power.

ABDOMINAL HOLLOW AND BRACE

Purpose: To activate the abdominal muscles. Abdominal hollowing and bracing, a key feature of all movement strength drills, is essential to effective stabilization of the trunk, particularly the lower back. Effectively performing this movement enhances core stability.

Procedure

1. Position yourself on your hands and knees, with your knees under your hips and your back relaxed in a neutral position.

2. Gently hollow the abdominal muscles below the navel without moving your lower back. This involves drawing the lower part of your belly back and slightly up, as if you are "scooping" it toward your spine. Then, progressively brace the remainder of your abdominal muscles as though you are about to be punched in the stomach.

3. Maintain this position for five seconds, rest for five seconds, and repeat for 5 sets.

Key points

- Breathe normally.
- Squeeze your buttocks if it helps you to hollow and brace.
- Vary your level of exertion between 30 and 90 percent effort. For all movement drills, exert sufficient effort to activate the key stabilizing muscles—that is, match the effort to the demands of the movement.

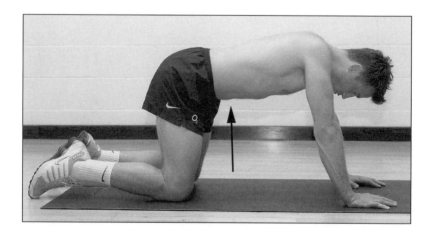

BENT KNEE TO SKY

Purpose: To activate the muscles of the buttocks, particularly the gluteus medius. This muscle helps to stabilize the hips and helps players maintain their balance during multidirectional running and contact. Strong and active gluteus medius muscles also reduce the chances of groin, knee, and hamstring injuries by supporting the hips.

Procedure

1. Lie on your side with your knees bent. Hollow and brace your abdominal muscles to maintain a neutral lower-back position.

2. Keeping your heels together, slowly lift the top knee by turning your hip out without letting your back or pelvis twist. Move only as far as you can without destabilizing your back and pelvis; there should be no movement in your lower back. Maintain control as you slowly return to the start position.

3. Raise your knee over a three-second period, hold for one second, and lower it to the start position over a count of three seconds. Perform three sets of 10 repetitions on each side, with no rest between sets.

Key points

- Breathe normally.
- Squeeze the buttock of the active leg.
- Focus on having your buttock muscles generate the movement.

TEARDROP SQUEEZE

Purpose: To activate the "teardrop" muscle (the vastus medialis oblique, or VMO). This very important knee-joint stabilizer helps the patella (kneecap) track correctly and reduces the likelihood of ligament injury and patella tendon inflammation.

Procedure

1. Sit on the floor with your legs slightly spread. Place a cushion or rugby ball under one knee and rotate your leg slightly toward the outside.

2. Push your knee down into the cushion or ball, which will raise your foot off the floor. Focus on the VMO, which runs down the front of the thigh to the inside of your kneecap.

3. Hold the position for 5 seconds, relax, and repeat for five squeezes. Repeat with the other leg. Perform three sets of five repetitions with 30 seconds' rest between sets.

Key point: Breathe normally.

T RAISES

Purpose: To activate the shoulder muscles that help to stabilize the shoulder joint. These muscles, particularly the lower trapezius muscles, help support the shoulder-joint complex when the arms are moving against resistance, as they do during a tackle. Having a stable shoulder complex makes contact movement patterns more effective and reduces the chance of shoulder injuries.

Procedure

1. Lie facedown with your arms in a T position (extended perpendicular to your trunk) and your palms facing the floor.
2. Pull your shoulder blades down, then raise your arms four to six inches off the floor. Keep your neck straight and look at the floor during the exercise.
3. Raise your arms over a count of 3 seconds, hold for 3 seconds, and lower them over a count of 3 seconds. Perform three sets of 10 repetitions with 45 seconds' rest between sets.

Key points

- Breathe normally.
- Squeeze the muscles between and around your shoulder blades.
- Keep your shoulders and upper trapezius muscles lowered, away from your ears.

DEEP NECK

Purpose: To activate the deep stabilizing muscles of the neck. Having a strong and controlled neck is vital during the many collisions in rugby.

Procedure

1. Lie on your back with your knees bent. Press your tongue against the roof of your mouth, pull your chin in toward your neck, and lift your head a few inches from the floor.

2. Hold for 5 seconds, then lower your head to the floor, still keeping your chin tucked in. Rest for 5 seconds, then repeat for a total of six holds.

Key points

• Breathe normally.

• Press your tongue against the roof of your mouth.

SQUAT AND SQUEEZE

Purpose: To activate the buttocks, thigh adductor, and teardrop muscles. These muscles work together to support high-intensity multidirectional running.

Procedure

1. Gradually squat over a period of three seconds so that your thighs are parallel with the floor, with your back against a wall or a Swiss ball. Place a ball or cushion between your knees.

2. Hold this position for five seconds, then remove the ball or cushion and return to a standing position over three seconds. Rest for five seconds, then repeat for a set of six holds.

Key point: Consciously activate your gluteus muscles and squeeze your knees together.

STATIC CORE STABILIZATION DRILLS

In static core stabilization drills, control and tension are generated in the key stabilizing muscles of the trunk.

LEG RAISE AND SUPPORT

Purpose: To activate the core stabilizing muscles of the abdomen. The benefits of core stability are listed on pages 71-72.

Procedure

1. Lie on your back with both knees bent and your feet together. Place your hands flat under the small of your back.
2. Gently hollow then brace the abdominal muscles and sustain this contraction without moving your lower back. Slowly raise one leg off the floor until your thigh is vertical to the floor, again without moving your lower back or pelvis and focusing on supporting the foot's movement with your abdominal muscles. Use your hands to feel for any changes in your lower-back position.
3. Hold for 5 seconds and slowly return to the start position.
4. Do five repetitions with each leg. Rest for 30 seconds, then repeat for three sets.

Key points

- Breathe normally and imagine pulling your belly toward your spine.
- Focus on maintaining a neutral spine.
- Use the minimum amount of effort possible.
- Focus on the deep muscles of the abdominal wall.

ARM AND LEG RAISE

Purpose: To develop the control and stabilizing qualities of the core stabilizers. This drill challenges several key muscles, including those in the abdomen, buttocks, and lower back.

Procedure

1. Position yourself on your hands and knees with your knees under your hips, your hands under your shoulders, and your back relaxed in a neutral position.

2. Hollow then brace the abdomen. Slowly raise one arm, extending it straight in front of you, and the opposite knee, straightening your hip and knee to extend the leg behind you. Slightly contract your buttocks during the leg lift. Do not let your back arch or twist, and try to get your arm and leg parallel with the ground. Lift them only as far as you can without losing a neutral back.

3. Hold for 5 seconds, then slowly lower both limbs to the start position. Repeat with the other arm and leg. Do three sets of five repetitions on each side, resting for 1 minute between sets.

Key points

- Keep your back in the same position from start to finish. Imagine that you are balancing a glass of wine on your lower back.

- Keep your shoulder blades low, away from your ears.

- Breathe normally.

ROTATING RAMP

Purpose: To develop the control and stabilizing qualities of the core stabilizers. The drill is performed in four separate positions.

Procedure

1. Prone Ramp. Lie facedown with your forearms on the ground beside your head. Raise your body off the floor by pushing down into the floor with your elbows and toes to assume the Prone Ramp position. Hold for 5 to 10 seconds, then bend your knees and return to the floor.

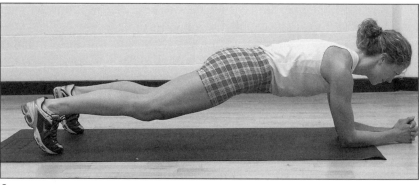

a

2. Side Ramp (left-side support). Rotate onto your left side so that your legs are straight and your weight is on your elbow. Hold for 5 to 10 seconds before returning to the floor.

b

3. Supine Ramp. Roll over onto your back and perform the drill in a supine position by raising yourself off the floor with your feet and elbows. Again, hold for 5 to 10 seconds before returning to the floor.

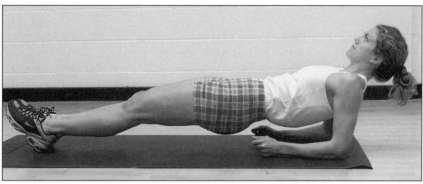

c

4. Side Ramp (right-side support). Finally, repeat the Side Ramp, but use your right elbow for support.

5. Perform this sequence three times. Do three sets of three repetitions, resting for 45 seconds between sets.

Key points

- Hollow then brace your abdomen in all the positions.
- Squeeze your buttocks for support.
- Keep your shoulders low, away from your ears.
- Try to proceed to the next position without returning to the floor.
- Stop performing the drill if you start shaking; the movement must be smooth and controlled.

SINGLE-LEG BRIDGE

Purpose: To develop the control and stabilizing qualities of the core stabilizers, particularly those in the buttocks. Rugby players commonly have weak and underactive buttocks, which often leads to excessive strain on the lower back and hamstrings. This drill helps to reverse this muscle imbalance. Because the buttock of the supporting leg has to support the other leg, stability and control are developed for running, split squatting, and lunging.

Procedure

1. Lie on your back with your knees bent and your feet together. Hollow then brace your abdomen, squeeze both buttocks, and push down into the floor with both feet to raise your hips off the floor.

2. From this position, slowly lift one foot off the floor and straighten the leg while keeping your back neutral. Do not let your back sag or your hips rotate. Hold for 5 seconds, then slowly and with control return to the start position. Repeat with the opposite leg.

3. Perform the 5-second holds five times with each leg. This equals one set. Do three sets with 30 seconds' rest between sets.

Key points

- Keep your knees together and your trunk immobile.
- Focus on squeezing the buttock of the supporting leg.

a

b

DYNAMIC CORE STABILIZATION DRILLS

Dynamic core drills are more challenging because they involve either moving or preventing movement on an unstable surface such as a Swiss ball. The unstable surface creates a dynamic environment that challenges the core stabilizing muscles.

SWISS BALL MAUL

Purpose: To develop dynamic core stability on an unstable surface with partner resistance. This drill will assist the player in applying static holding strength to prevent the release of the ball.

Procedure

1. Lie supine on a Swiss ball with your knees bent, your feet flat on the floor, and a rugby ball hugged to your chest. Try to achieve neutral alignment.

2. Hollow and brace your abdomen and activate your gluteus muscles. Try to remain stable as your partner pushes you on the Swiss ball and attempts to pull the rugby ball from your grasp. Start with light pushing and pulling and vary the angle of the maul.

3. Perform for 10 seconds with 10 seconds' rest afterward. Repeat for five sets.

Key points

- Progress to random changes in pressure, and close your eyes!
- Breathe normally.

PRONE EXTENSIONS

Purpose: To develop the lower-back muscles. This is an excellent drill for recruiting and developing the small lower-back muscles (the multifidus) close to the spine. The drill develops extension strength, an element that helps prevent lower-back pain.

Procedure

1. Lie with your belly on a Swiss ball and your feet secured or pressed against a wall.

2. Let your head and chest curl down over the ball, then slowly, over a period of 3 seconds, curl back up to a neutral spine position. Hold this position for 3 seconds and curl back down over 3 seconds.

3. Do this 10 times, then rest for 60 seconds. Then do two more sets.

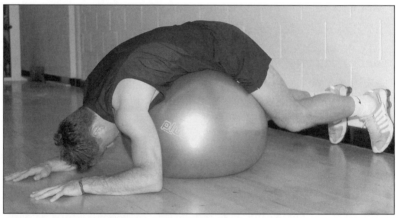

a

b

Key points

- Never go beyond a neutral spine position.
- Focus on curling down and then up so that your back is allowed to flex and extend gradually.

Progression

- Move the Swiss ball closer to your waist.
- Hold a light weight—for example, a 1-kilogram dumbbell—in both hands.
- Hold a light weight in just one hand to load just one side of the lumbar spine.

OFF-LOAD ROTATION

Purpose: To develop dynamic stability during rotation. This drill mimics the stability demands of off-loading in contact to teach the correct muscles to stabilize the body.

Procedure

1. Lie supine on a Swiss ball with your knees bent at 90 degrees and your feet flat on the floor. Try to achieve neutral alignment. Hold a rugby ball at arm's-length above your chest.

2. Slowly roll your head, shoulders, and arms to one side, rotating with the rugby ball to simulate a pass and allowing the Swiss ball to roll slightly in the opposite direction. Go only as far as you can while still maintaining control and keeping your pelvis level.

3. Rotate over a period of 3 seconds, hold for 3 seconds at the farthest point of the rotation, and then return with control over 3 seconds. Do five repetitions to each side, rest for 60 seconds, and repeat the set two more times.

a

b

Key points

- Push up with the buttock on the side you're moving the ball toward to keep your hips from following your shoulders.

- Focus on controlling the movement with your abdominal muscles.

- Do not use momentum to roll from side to side.

NECK STABILIZER

Purpose: To develop the muscles that help to stabilize the neck. Neck stability is crucial in a contact sport like rugby.

Procedure

1. Kneel in front of a Swiss ball that rests against a wall or your partner. Resting your arms on the ball for support, lean forward and place your forehead on the ball so that your arms and head are sharing your body's weight.

2. While maintaining a neutral head position, press your tongue against the roof of your mouth and slowly redirect the weight passing through your arms to your head to challenge your neck muscles. If your head starts shaking, you have allowed too much weight to go through your head. Hold this position for 10 seconds.

3. Repeat the drill three more times, then rest for 60 seconds and repeat for three sets.

Key point: Resist the temptation to thrust your chin forward.

Progression

- Raise one arm slightly off the ball.
- Rotate the ball from side to side with your hands so that your head moves slightly to the left and then to the right, but not up or down.

Dan's Top Tip

Neck strength is very similar to core stability strength. The aim is to train the neck to withstand the impact of a scrum, maul, or tackle to provide a solid platform for your head and shoulders. The focus is on training the neck muscles to be stable, and the neck should not be craned at various angles.

SHOULDER STEP-UP

Purpose: To develop the stabilizers of the shoulders while demanding support from the leg and trunk muscles. This drill improves shoulder stability and helps to reduce the incidence of shoulder injuries.

Procedure

1. Assume the push-up position in front of a small step of approximately 20 centimeters high. Focus on maintaining a stable trunk by hollowing and bracing your abdomen and squeezing your buttocks.

2. Use your hands to step up onto and down from the step in this sequence: left hand up, right hand up, left hand down, right hand down. This is 1 repetition.

3. Do 10 repetitions of step 2, leading with the left hand 5 times and then with the right hand. Repeat for four sets, with 90 seconds' rest between sets.

Key points

- Keep your trunk neutral throughout the movement.
- Focus on keeping your trapezius muscles away from your ears and your shoulder blades fixed.

Progression: Raise one leg a short distance off the floor during the drill.

PUSH-UP AND PULL

Purpose: To develop the stabilizers of the trunk and shoulders. This drill introduces trunk rotation and mimics the frequent twists and turns performed during such movements as tackling and mauling.

Procedure

1. Assume the push-up position, hollow then brace your abdomen, and squeeze your buttocks to help you maintain a stable trunk.

2. Take one hand off the floor and raise it vertically as far as you can before losing control. Allow your feet and legs to rotate with your

a

b

arm. Raise the arm over a period of 3 seconds, hold it there for 1 second, and lower it over 3 seconds. After returning to the start position, repeat the movement with the other arm to equal one repetition.

3. Perform three repetitions with each arm, then rest for 60 seconds. Do four sets.

Key point: Keep your supporting shoulder stable by pulling it down away from your ear and bracing the surrounding muscles.

Progression: Perform a standard push-up between each arm raise.

PATTERN STRENGTH DRILLS

These drills use rugby movements such as lunging and squatting to strengthen the body and teach it how to move correctly. Drills should be performed only with the body's weight and within a controllable range of motion. Hold a rugby ball while doing these drills to increase the specificity of the movements.

After several weeks of pattern drill training, once you feel confident performing three sets of 15 repetitions for each drill, load your body by wearing a 10-kilogram weighted vest or holding a 3- to 5-kilogram medicine ball. Do not increase the load any more than that until you have completed a phase of loaded strength drills.

LUNGE AND DUMMY PASS

Purpose: To develop functional strength for the movement pattern of lunging and twisting. A dummy pass is the performance of a passing movement without releasing the ball. This drill prepares you for rugby stepping and twisting movements like passing, catching, and off-loading in contact.

Procedure

1. At a walking pace, lunge forward with your right leg until your thigh is parallel with the ground or as low as you can get it while still being in control (but no lower than parallel). At the same time, twist your upper body to the right (over the leading leg) and dummy-pass the ball. Then twist your upper body to the left and dummy-pass to the left. Make these movements over a period of three seconds.

2. Return to the start position and repeat the drill, this time lunging with the left leg.

Key point: Focus on controlling the movement with the core stabilizing muscles by hollowing and bracing the abdomen and squeezing the buttocks.

Progression: Release the ball to a partner and hold the end position for the return pass.

MULTIDIRECTIONAL LUNGE

Purpose: To develop functional leg strength at multiple movement angles. Rugby movements involve numerous angles, including forward, lateral, backward, and others of various degrees. This drill teaches and strengthens the muscles responsible for generating these patterns.

Procedure: There are four distinct lunging movements: forward, sideways (right), backward, and sideways (left).

1. Forward Lunge. At walking pace, lunge forward with your right leg until the thigh is either parallel with the ground or as low as you can get it while still being in control (but no lower than parallel). Hold the position for 2 seconds, then repeat the movement with your left leg. Return to the start position.

2. Side Lunge (right and left). Repeat step 1, but lunge to your right and place your body weight on your right leg before holding for

a   b

2 seconds and then pushing back to the start position. Lunge again, but to the left, and then return to the start position.

3. Backward Lunge. Lunge backward with your right leg until the left thigh is parallel with the ground. Hold for 2 seconds. Then, use the left leg to generate the movement that returns you to the start position. Repeat, but lunge backward with the left leg.

4. One set equals three repetitions of this sequence: left and right Forward Lunges, left and right Side Lunges, and left and right Backward Lunges. Perform four sets, allowing 60 seconds' rest between sets.

Key points

- Ensure that the knee of the leading leg does not go beyond the toes.
- Focus on controlling the movement with the core stabilizing muscles.

Progression

- Repeat the sequence, but add lunges at other angles; imagine that you are lunging around a clockface, stepping toward the numerals.
- Twist your upper body to replicate the Lunge and Dummy Pass drill.

SINGLE-LEG SQUAT AND DUMMY PASS

Purpose: To develop functional leg strength. This movement isolates one leg and requires support from the trunk muscles. The dummy pass introduces rotation and replicates the strength demands of rugby.

Procedure

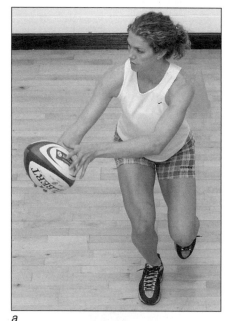

1. Stand on one leg while holding a rugby ball with both hands.

2. Over a period of 2 seconds, lower yourself to a half squat or whatever depth you are able to control. Then dummy-pass first to the right and then to the left (figure *a*). Return to the start position over 2 seconds, then change legs and repeat.

3. Repeat for three sets of eight squats on each leg, resting for 60 seconds between sets.

a

This drill can also be performed as a single-leg deadlift. Stand on one slightly bent leg and flex forward at the hips. Once you reach a manageable range (do not allow your torso to go beyond parallel with the ground), perform dummy passes to the left and right (figure *b*). Return to the start position and repeat while standing on the other leg.

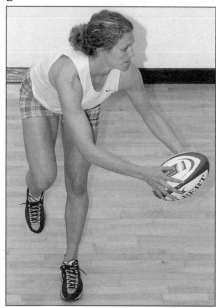

Key points

- Do not let your knee go beyond your toes.

- Focus on controlling the movement with the buttock of the squatting leg.

b

REACH AND TOUCH DOWN

Purpose: To develop functional leg strength. This drill incorporates all of the elements of functional strength—flexion, rotation, extension, and deceleration—and prepares players for the reaching and bending movements performed during rugby.

Procedure

1. Stand with your feet at shoulder-width apart and hold a rugby ball above your head.

2. Over a period of 2 seconds, lunge forward, keeping your chest behind your leading knee, and gradually reach down to touch the ball to the floor to the outside of your foot. Allow your rear leg to flex nearly to the ground (but not to contact it) to gain depth with the lunge. Hold for 2 seconds.

3. Return to the start position over 2 seconds and repeat, leading with the other leg.

4. Do three sets of six lunges with each leg, resting for 60 seconds between sets.

Key points

- Do not let your knee go beyond your toes.
- Focus on controlling the movement with the core stabilizing muscles.

LATERAL WALL SQUAT

Purpose: To develop functional leg strength. This drill strengthens the leg muscles used to support the body in a leaning position, improving the player's ability to change direction while running.

Procedure

1. Stand sidelong to a Swiss ball held between your flexed elbow and a wall.

2. Lean against the ball at an angle of approximately 30 degrees, supporting your weight with the outside leg. Keeping your hips and shoulders squared as you lean on the ball, lower yourself into a squat over a period of 3 seconds. Because of your downward movement, the ball will eventually be repositioned against your shoulder. Squat only as low as you can go without losing control and hold for 1 second.

a

3. Straighten your hips and knees to return to the start position over 2 seconds. Repeat the exercise while facing the other direction so that you use the opposite leg.

4. Do six squats with each leg for one set. Perform three sets with 90 seconds' rest between sets.

Key points

- Maintain neutral body alignment.

- Push the foot of the weight-bearing leg into the ground.

b

SUPINE MAUL-UP

Purpose: To develop functional pulling strength. This challenging exercise develops the muscles responsible for pulling actions, like mauling a ball and wrestling opponents.

Procedure

1. Lie supine on the floor with your feet flat and your hands grasping a bar that is safely supported above your chest in a squat rack. Straighten your trunk and legs, hollow and brace your abdomen, and squeeze your buttocks.

a

b

2. As you breathe out, pull yourself toward the bar over a period of two seconds, focusing on maintaining a solid torso and lowering your shoulders away from your ears. Hold for one second, then breathe in as you descend to the start position over two seconds.

3. Repeat until you feel unable to complete the full range of movement. Rest for two minutes and repeat for three sets.

Key point: Maintain neutral body alignment.

Progression: Perform a single-arm supine pull-up that mimics the movement performed during the Push-Up and Pull drill. While holding onto the bar with one hand, allow your body to rotate toward the floor, then rotate back up.

MULTICHOP

Purpose: The Multichop drill integrates the qualities of functional movement. It develops strength in motion by moving between two extremes—reaching up and across to simulate catching a high ball or lineout and flexing down and across to simulate offloading and mauling.

Procedure

1. With both hands, hold a rugby ball above your head and off to one side, keeping your feet slightly wider apart than shoulder width.

2. Over a period of two seconds, flex and rotate the ball down to the knee on the opposite side and hold for two seconds. Then return over two seconds to the start position by extending your arms back over your head and to the side. Hold there

a

b

for two seconds. Allow your trunk to curl as you flex and extend and your feet and knees to follow the ball as you flex downward.

3. Do three sets of five repetitions on each side, resting for one minute between sets.

Key point: Allow your feet and knees to move naturally with the ball.

Progression: Once you feel that you have mastered this drill, chop to the ankle instead of the knee.

LOADED STRENGTH DRILLS

Loaded strength training focuses on traditional resistance drills that allow you to load muscle groups through a linear plane of motion.

Loaded upper-body drills should first be performed with a barbell and then, after several weeks or when you are able to, with a dumbbell. Movements made with dumbbells require greater control and are more specific to rugby than are those executed with a barbell. You can then progress to alternating single-arm lifting and ultimately to single-arm lifting.

Tempo and Load

These are strength—not speed strength—drills. Movements should be not fast, but rather controlled, and should pass through the full available range of motion. Never exercise to failure, only to fatigue, and do not attempt to lift unrealistic loads. Begin with two or three sets of 8 to 12 repetitions using a comfortable load and allow two minutes' rest between sets.

Breathing

Breathing correctly is vital for distributing oxygenated blood to the muscles. During high-effort lifting, such as a Weighted Push-Up, the lifter should inhale prior to and during the lowering (recovery) phase and exhale during the lifting (exertion) phase. Holding your breath for too long raises your blood pressure and restricts blood flow, potentially causing dizziness and loss of control.

Spotting

Guiding and spotting are crucial for all loaded strength exercises. Lifters are commonly spotted during a Bench Press, but how often do you see someone being spotted during a pull-up, squat, or Bent-Over Row? In all cases, the spotter can provide feedback on body alignment and technique while also being available to assist the player with lifting if he or she becomes fatigued or loses control.

Developing a Technique Base

A good technique base should be developed several weeks before loaded strength drills are introduced. For example, movements such as the squat should be rehearsed using a bar or broom handle and evaluated by a professional. Never sacrifice technique for a greater load or faster movement. All exercises are hazardous if they are performed incorrectly, and having perfect technique is your goal.

BACK SQUAT

Purpose: To develop strength in the buttocks and thighs. This movement involves the extension of the ankles, knees, and hips and is an excellent way to develop general strength for almost all of the movement patterns of rugby. The squat also develops the stabilizing muscles of the hips and knees, which helps to protect those areas from injury.

Procedure

1. In a standing position, grip and rest the bar across your shoulders at the base of your neck. Your feet should be set slightly wider than shoulder-width apart with your toes pointing slightly outward. Hollow and brace your abdomen and hold your chest up and out.

2. For the two- to three-second downward phase, allow your hips and knees to slowly flex while you maintain a neutral spine and keep your feet flat on the floor. Continue to flex until your thighs are parallel with the floor or you have lowered yourself as far as your flexibility allows you to when your spine is neutral. Align your knees over your feet.

3. In the upward phase, return to the start position over two to three seconds by extending your hips and knees at the same rate and keeping your back flat and your chest high.

Key points

- Use at least one spotter during this lift.
- Squeeze your buttocks as you begin the upward phase.
- Do not bounce as you complete either phase.

FRONT SQUAT

Purpose: To develop strength in the buttocks and thighs. This drill has benefits similar to those of the back squat, and it emphasizes the front of the thighs and challenges the abdominal muscles.

Procedure

1. In a standing position, grip and rest the bar across your upper chest, holding it with your arms either parallel or crossed. Your feet should be set slightly wider than shoulder-width apart, with your toes pointing slightly outward. Hollow and brace your abdomen and hold your chest up and out.

2. For the two- to three-second downward phase, allow your hips and knees to slowly flex while you keep your back flat and your feet flat on the floor. Continue to flex until your thighs are parallel with the floor or you have lowered yourself as far as your flexibility allows you to when your spine is neutral. Align your knees over your feet.

3. In the upward phase, return to the start position over two to three seconds by extending your hips and knees at the same rate and maintaining a flat back and high chest.

Key points

- Use at least one spotter during this lift.
- Note the increased support you get from your abdominal muscles compared to their effect during the back squat.
- Squeeze your buttocks as you start the upward phase.
- Do not bounce as you complete either phase.

BENCH PRESS

Purpose: To develop strength in the chest, shoulders, and arms. Although the Bench Press has little benefit to shoulder stability (because the bench acts as the shoulder stabilizers), this drill develops general pushing strength and improves such movements as rising from the ground and handing off opponents. Shoulder Step-Ups and Weighted Push-Ups must be included in the training program to develop functional pushing strength.

Procedure

1. Lie supine on a bench with your eyes in line with the supports and your feet flat on the floor. Place your hands on the bar at slightly wider than shoulder-width apart. Make sure that your trunk is neutral. Hollow and brace your abdomen.

2. Lower the bar over two to three seconds to your chest at the nipples, keeping your wrists rigid, your feet on the floor, and your shoulders and hips on the bench.

3. Over a two- to three-second period, raise the bar to the supports by pressing it upward on a slight arc until your elbows are extended.

Key points

- Use at least one spotter during this lift.
- Do not arch your back so that it rises off the bench.
- Do not bounce as you complete either phase.
- Concentrate on pulling your shoulder blades together at the end of the movement.
- Tall players can place their feet on a raised platform to help them maintain a neutral lumbar spine.

BENT-OVER ROW

Purpose: To develop strength in the back and shoulders. This exercise improves pulling strength, which is important to activities such as mauling and wrestling opponents. The movement also requires the static support of the legs and trunk.

Procedure

1. From a semisquat position, place your hands on the bar at more than shoulder-width apart. Hollow and brace your abdomen to make sure your trunk is neutral.

2. Over a period of two seconds, pull the bar up to your lower chest or upper abdomen with your elbows pointing up and your trunk rigid.

3. Lower the bar at the same rate by extending your elbows, but not changing the positions of your trunk or knees.

Key points

- Use at least one spotter during this lift.
- Do not jerk your trunk to assist you in this lift.

a

b

DEADLIFT

a

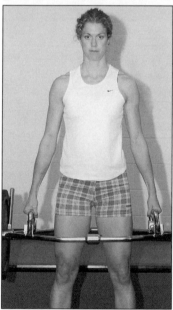

b

Purpose: To develop strength in the buttocks, thighs, and back. This advanced drill benefits general strength. Players *must* have a very sound strength base before attempting this drill. In addition, deadlifting should be done only with light to medium loads because of the stress the movement places on the lumbar spine. Do not progress to heavy loads and do not perform this exercise to fatigue.

Procedure

1. Start with your feet flat on the floor between hip- and shoulder-width apart, toes slightly outward. Squat and place your hands on the bar at slightly more than shoulder-width apart. Your shoulders should be slightly ahead of the bar. Hollow and brace your abdomen to make sure your trunk is neutral.

2. Extend your hips and knees to lift the bar from the floor over a period of two to three seconds. Keep the bar as close to your body as possible. As the bar passes your knees, move your hips forward so that your thighs meet the bar. Continue the upward movement until you stand erect. *Do not extend your back beyond neutral at the end of the movement.*

3. Return to the start position over three seconds by lowering the bar slowly as you flex your hips and knees, maintaining a neutral back at all times.

Key points

- Do not let your hips rise before your shoulders do.
- Keep your arms straight.

HAMSTRING PENDULUM

Purpose: To develop hamstring strength. This important drill helps to prevent hamstring muscle tears and strains, which are among the most common rugby injuries. The drill replicates the eccentric (lengthening) movement associated with high-speed running and deceleration. It is a difficult drill, so be patient: Do not expect to achieve much range, and be prepared for postexercise stiffness in the hamstring when you introduce it into your program.

Procedure: Kneel on a soft surface with your feet anchored by a partner or bench. Keeping your trunk straight, slowly lean forward to a manageable distance before slowly returning to the start position.

Key points

- Avoid flexing at the hips.
- At first, you may need to put your hands down after leaning forward to assist with returning to the start point.

Dan's Top Tip

This is an excellent drill for strengthening the hamstrings and preventing hamstring injuries. Include it in your program all year long.

SHOULDER PRESS

Purpose: To develop strength in the shoulders. This drill specifically assists with lineout lifting and also with general shoulder strength.

Procedure

1. Stand with your knees slightly flexed and the bar resting across your shoulders with your hands set at slightly more than shoulder-width apart. Look directly ahead of you to encourage a neutral neck, and keep your feet flat on the floor. Raise the bar over your head by pressing the bar upward until your elbows are extended. Hollow and brace your abdomen to make sure your trunk is neutral, and do not arch your back.

2. Over two seconds, lower the bar to touch the front of your shoulders, keeping your wrists rigid.

Key Points

• Use at least one spotter during this lift.

a

b

- Do not extend your back beyond neutral as you press upward to raise the bar.

Progression

Flex then extend your knees as you press the bar. This generates momentum from your legs and is termed a push press.

WEIGHTED PUSH-UP

Purpose: To develop strength in the chest, shoulders, and arms. Unlike the Bench Press, the Weighted Push-Up challenges the muscles that stabilize the shoulder joint during movements generated by the arm and chest muscles.

Procedure: Do a standard push-up, but increase the resistance by wearing a weighted vest or having a partner balance and support a weight on your upper back. Descend over two to three seconds and return to the start position at the same tempo. Use push-up handles, because the increased load places too much stress on your wrists if your hands are flat on the floor.

Key points

- Use at least one spotter during this exercise.
- Do not arch your back; instead, keep your body alignment neutral throughout the exercise.
- Do not bounce when you return to the start position.

Progression: Increase the load on your chest, arms, and shoulders by elevating your feet.

FRONT AND LATERAL RAISES

Purpose: To increase shoulder strength. The front raise develops the anterior deltoid muscles (the front of the shoulders) and the lateral raise develops the medial deltoid muscles (the lateral shoulders). Both drills improve strength for contact movements.

Procedure

1. Stand with your feet shoulder-width apart, with your arms hanging at your sides and holding a dumbbell in each hand with an overhand grip. Over a period of two to three seconds, raise the dumbbells upward and forward (front raise) or upward and sideways (lateral raise) until the dumbbells are level with your shoulders.

2. Lower the dumbbells over two to three seconds.

Key points

- Do not arch your back; instead, keep your body alignment neutral throughout the exercise.

- Do not bounce at the end of either the lifting or lowering phase.

ALTERNATIVE LOADED STRENGTH DRILLS

The loaded strength drills you've just read about work all the major muscle groups. However, many other movements can be loaded by using dumbbells or barbells, such as bodyweight dips, which involve lowering and raising the body using the arms and shoulders, and bicep curls, a traditional exercise that isolates the bicep muscles and involves flexing and extending the arm while holding a dumbbell. Various cable pulley drills are also worth considering for inclusion in your loaded strength program.

POWER DRILLS

All of the movement and loaded drills covered so far in this book provide the foundation for your power drill training. Power drills must not be performed until a phase of movement and loaded strength training has been completed.

A key principle in performing all power drills is getting adequate rest between sets. The nervous and energy systems responsible for generating powerful movements fatigue relatively quickly and require several minutes to recover. Depending on the demands of the drill, the rest time between sets needs to be three to five minutes long.

EXPLOSIVE LIFTING DRILLS

In these movements, sometimes referred to as *Olympic lifts*, the simultaneous extension of the ankle, knee, and hip joints generates the movement of the load (a barbell or dumbbell). This triple extension is used in most rugby movements, including acceleration, scrummaging, lineout lifting, jumping, and tackling. As a result, these drills are very popular with elite players, who have the time and supervision to develop correct technique for explosive lifting.

Dan's Top Tip

Develop your technique for explosive lifting drills by simulating the movements with a broom handle early in your training program. Don't expect overnight miracles from explosive lifting, and try to concentrate on technique rather than the amount of weight being lifted. Work on technique with an expert instructor first and then go for a slow progression in weight.

POWER PULL

Purpose: To develop explosive speed strength (power). The aim of the drill is to forcefully pull the bar from the floor to the chest in one dynamic movement.

Procedure

1. Stand with your feet flat and set between hip- and shoulder-width apart. Point your toes slightly outward. Squat and place your hands on the bar at slightly wider than shoulder-width apart with your arms fully extended. Your shoulders should be above or slightly past the bar in front of you, and the bar should be just a few centimeters from your shins. Hollow and brace your abdomen to support your trunk.

2. Upward phase 1: Begin by lifting the bar off the floor by extending your hips and knees while maintaining a flat back and high chest. Keep the bar as close as possible to your shins.

a

3. Upward phase 2: Once the bar reaches your knees, rapidly thrust your hips forward so that your thighs meet the bar.

4. Upward phase 3: Continue the rapid movement by forcing your hips, knees, and ankles to extension while keeping the bar as close as possible to your body. As these joints reach full extension, quickly shrug your shoulders upward while keeping your elbows extended.

5. Upward phase 4: When the shrug reaches maximum height, use this momentum to rapidly flex your elbows and pull the bar up to chest height, focusing on bringing your elbows up high.

b

6. Downward phase: Allow your hips and knees to slowly flex while you keep your back flat and your feet flat on the floor. Slowly lower the bar with control to your thighs and then, with fully extended elbows, to the floor as you squat down. Lowering the bar should take two to three seconds.

Key point: Focus on pressing your feet into the floor to generate the maximum reaction during upward stages 2 through 4.

POWER CLEAN

Purpose: To develop explosive speed strength (power). The aim of the drill is to forcefully pull the bar from the floor to your shoulders in one dynamic movement. The movement is very similar to the Power Pull except for the upward catch phase (upward phase 4).

Procedure

1. Stand with your feet flat and set between hip- and shoulder-width apart. Point your toes slightly outward. Squat and place your hands on the bar at slightly wider than shoulder-width apart with your arms fully extended. Your shoulders should be above or slightly beyond the bar in front of you, and the bar should be just a few centimeters from your shins. Hollow and brace your abdomen to support your trunk. Upward phases 1, 2, and 3 are the same as in the Power Pull.

2. Upward phase 4 (catch phase): As the bar reaches maximum height, dip the hips and knees into a semisquat position to position your body under the bar, and then rapidly rotate your arms to catch it. Try to get your upper arms parallel with the floor as you start extending your hips and knees to reach a fully extended, erect posture.

3. Downward phase: Allow your hips and knees to slowly flex while keeping your back flat and your feet flat on the floor. Slowly lower the bar with control to your thighs and then, with fully extended arms, to the floor as you squat down. Lowering the bar should take two or three seconds.

Key point: Focus on pressing your feet into the floor to generate the maximum reaction during upward stages 2 through 4.

POWER SNATCH

Purpose: To develop explosive speed strength (power). The aim of the drill is to forcefully pull the bar from the floor to above your head in one dynamic movement.

Procedure

1. Stand with your feet flat and set between hip- and shoulder-width apart. Point your toes slightly outward. Squat and place your hands on the bar relatively far apart compared with where they are for the Power Pull or Power Clean. The recommended distance is where your elbows would be if your arms were extended straight out at your sides. Your shoulders should be above or slightly beyond the bar in front of you, and the bar should be just a few centimeters from your shins. With your eyes focused straight ahead of you, hollow and brace your abdomen to support your trunk.

2. Upward phase 1: Begin by lifting the bar off the floor by extending your hips and knees while maintaining a flat back and high chest.

a

Keep the bar as close as possible to your shins.

3. Upward phase 2: Once the bar reaches your knees, rapidly thrust your hips forward so that your thighs meet the bar for a split second.

4. Upward phase 3: Continue the rapid movement by forcing your hips, knees, and ankles to extension while keeping the bar as close as possible to your body. As these joints reach full extension, quickly shrug your shoulders upward and then flex your elbows to begin moving your body under the bar.

b

5. Upward phase 4 (catch phase): As the bar reaches near-maximum height, pull your body under it and then rapidly rotate your arms to catch it. At the same time, dip your hips and knees into a

semisquat position. Try to catch the bar with your fully extended arms and then return to a fully erect posture by extending your hips and knees. Hold the bar stable overhead for one to two seconds.

6. Downward phase: Lower the bar from above your head by bending your arms. Allow your hips and knees to slowly flex as you keep your back flat and your feet flat on the floor. Slowly lower the bar with control to your thighs and then, with fully extended arms, to the floor as you squat down. Lowering the bar should take two or three seconds.

Key point: Focus on pressing your feet into the floor to generate the maximum reaction during upward stages 2 through 4.

Hang Options

The Power Pull, Power Clean, and Power Snatch can also be performed from a hang position. As you can see in the photo below, the start position is at the midthigh.

MEDICINE BALL DRILLS

Medicine balls are excellent power training tools. They allow you to perform dynamic and functional movements at various angles and high speeds. The drills here involve the rugby skills of catching and passing.

Start doing these drills with a three-kilogram medicine ball and progress to heavier balls as your speed strength improves. Don't forget—if the medicine ball is too heavy, the movement becomes a strength exercise as the speed of movement slows down.

CATCH, RELEASE, DROP, AND GO!

Purpose: To develop speed strength for catching, offloading, and rising from the ground.

Procedure

1. Stand approximately five meters away from your partner, who passes the medicine ball to you at chest height.

2. After you catch the ball, squat down quickly and then extend your hips and knees as you pass back the ball. As you release the ball, follow your forward momentum and drop to a front support position on the floor. Immediately push up and rise to your feet and sprint past your partner. Perform the drill as explosively as possible, but be sure to use correct technique and control.

a

b

3. Perform three sets of three repetitions with a one-minute rest between repetitions and four minutes between sets.

Progression: Receive the ball slightly to the left or right.

BACK TO WALL PASS AND CATCH

Purpose: To develop powerful rotation while passing and catching.

Procedure

1. Stand approximately three meters from a wall or partner, holding the ball with both of your hands at waist height and facing away from the wall or partner.

2. Turn your body by taking one step backward and twisting your trunk by 90 to 130 degrees. Allow your feet and knees to follow your trunk as you pivot on your feet. As you finish the turn, off-load the ball to the wall or partner and hold the position until the ball returns to you.

3. As you receive the ball, immediately return to the start position and repeat the drill in the opposite direction. Perform the drill as explosively as possible, but use correct technique and control.

4. Perform eight passes (four to each side) for one set. Allow maximum recovery time between additional sets.

SIDE TO WALL PASS AND TURN

Purpose: To develop powerful rotation and rapid foot movement while passing and catching.

Procedure

1. Stand sidelong to and approximately two meters from a wall or partner, holding the ball with both of your hands at waist height.

2. Pass the ball to the wall or your partner and use the momentum generated to follow through and jump 180 degrees around so that you land with your other side facing the wall. Allow your feet and knees to follow your trunk as you pivot on your outside foot, and angle your pass so that you can catch the ball as soon as you land.

3. As you receive the ball, resist the ball's momentum that takes it away from you, then immediately repeat the pass and jump movements to return to the start position. Perform the drill as explosively as possible, but use correct technique and control.

4. Perform eight passes (four to each side) for one set. Allow maximum recovery time between additional sets.

Key point: Focus on performing a fast rotational jump, not on the height of the jump.

Progression: Stand farther away from the wall.

PLYOMETRIC DRILLS

Plyometrics are jumps or combinations of jumps that produce quick, powerful movement using a *stretch reflex*. A stretch reflex occurs when a muscle lengthens (stretches) and then immediately shortens—the reflex action occurs when the muscle changes from the lengthening to the shortening action. These drills are a specific training mode for rugby because the movements replicate the game's mixture of vertical and horizontal acceleration against the ground and the triple extension of the ankle, knee, and hip joints.

Based on the heights and distances that the players are required to jump, the drills that follow are considered medium-intensity plyometric drills, and they should be introduced only after you have successfully completed a core stabilization, pattern strength, and loaded strength phase of training. You can begin doing these drills when you can do a Back Squat with one and a half times your body weight and 10 single-leg body-weight half squats on each leg with your eyes closed.

So that these drills will also help to prevent ankle and knee injuries, multidirectional movements are incorporated to reflect the multi-directional nature of rugby. These drills have a strong proprioceptive component (they challenge balance and the self-awareness of muscles and joints) and positively affect power, speed, agility, coordination, and stability strength.

Training Guidelines

- Perform plyometric drills only after reaching a satisfactory level of movement and loaded strength.
- Do not perform plyometrics more than twice per week or when tired.
- Try to land on the ball of your foot and flex and extend the ankles, knees, and hips during all jumps.
- Start with no more than 25 to 30 jumps per session and carefully follow the principle of progression.
- Start with double-leg jumps and progress to single-leg jumps. Keep feet shoulder-width apart and land on both feet at the same time.
- Use your arms to assist you in jumping and maintaining neutral body alignment.
- Do not perform depth jumps (drills that begin from a height).
- Do not perform these drills if you are suffering from a knee or ankle injury unless it is part of your supervised rehabilitation program.

JUMP AND FIX

Purpose: To develop reactive speed and stability strength. The hopping movement develops reactive speed strength and the final landing phase of the drill develops the stability strength necessary for decelerating and preventing knee and ankle injuries.

Equipment and area: Three mini hurdles (six inches high), placed 0.75 meter apart, and a surface that "gives," such as grass, a wooden floor, or a track.

Procedure

1. Perform three double-foot hops over the hurdles, landing on both feet between each hurdle, but on only one leg after the final hurdle. Try to stabilize your position on the single-leg landing to avoid any further forward or sideways movement. Repeat, but land on the opposite leg for one repetition.

2. Do three sets of three drills with three or four minutes' rest between sets.

Key points

- Do not let your knee go beyond your toes on the single-foot landing.

- Perform the drill slowly at first, but gradually reduce your contact time with the ground as you gain confidence.

Progression: Turn 90 degrees in the air as you hop over the final hurdle (advanced drill).

POSITIVE HOPS

Purpose: To develop multidirectional reactive speed strength.

Equipment and area: A one square meter plus sign marked with tape or marking spray, and a wooden or grassy surface.

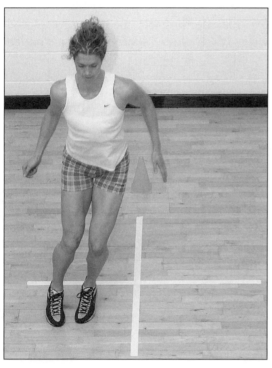

Procedure

1. Using both feet, hop clockwise around the +, landing between the lines, until you return to the starting position. Then, immediately change direction and hop counterclockwise back to the start position for one set.

2. Perform one set of jumps in each direction, rest for two minutes, then repeat for four sets.

Key points

- Always face forward so that you have to jump laterally and backward to reach some of the sectors.
- Aim for the middle of each sector and avoid landing close to the lines.
- Perform the drill slowly at first, but gradually reduce your contact time with the ground as you gain confidence.

Progression

- Jump over mini-hurdles instead of lines.
- Perform the drill hopping on one leg.

GRID CHALLENGE

Purpose: To develop multidirectional reactive speed and stability strength. This is an advanced drill.

Equipment and area: A grid of nine sectors, each measuring half a square meter, marked with tape or marking spray; a wooden or grassy surface; and a stopwatch.

Procedure

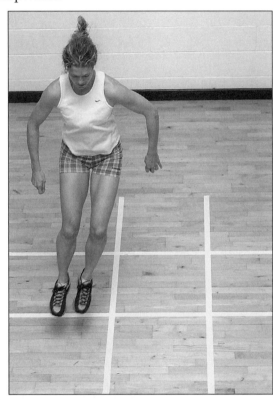

1. Starting in the center square, hop forward one sector and then clockwise around the grid on both feet, returning to the center square after each hop. Make sure your hips are facing forward at all times. Landing in the center square from the front left square completes one lap.

2. Change direction immediately and repeat the course going counterclockwise. Perform the drill slowly at first, but gradually reduce your contact time with the ground as you gain confidence.

3. Rest for three or four minutes, then repeat for three sets.

Key points

- Face forward on all jumps.
- Use a stopwatch to measure how long it takes to complete a lap in each direction.
- Do not touch any of the grid lines; apply a one-second penalty for each grid touch.

Progression: Perform the course by hopping on a single leg.

INTEGRATED STRENGTH AND POWER DRILLS

These advanced training drills involve rugby-specific movement patterns that require a blend of stability, strength, and explosive power. Perform these drills with maximum effort once you have rehearsed the appropriate technique.

TACKLE BREAKER!

Purpose: To develop dynamic strength for breaking through would-be tacklers. This drill adheres to the complex training system (see page 105), in which an exercise performed with a load (a sled) is repeated without a load.

Equipment and area: Loaded sled and two pad holders.

Procedure

1. Attach yourself to a sled loaded with 10 percent of your body weight and stand 10 meters from two pad holders.

2. Accelerate over the 10 meters and burst through the pad holders, who should offer a reasonable level of resistance. Maintain a low

body position and pump your legs through the contact and for 10 meters beyond.

3. Rest for 60 seconds and repeat the drill without the sled. Rest for four minutes, then repeat the drill for four to six sets.

Key points

- Apply maximum speed and maintain a forward-leaning body position.
- A weighted vest can be used instead of a weighted sled.
- A rugby ball can also be held during the drill.

Dan's Top Tip

Train to run through tacklers rather than into them. Don't aim for the middle of the tackler, set yourself up to change direction as you come into contact with him or her. Try to draw defenders' eyes away from your legs: If they aren't looking at your legs, they won't know where you are going to go. You are bound to lose your balance during contact, but if you train yourself to quickly move away from the situation—with quick feet and your body and weight angled forward—then you are likely to get the better of the situation.

TURNOVER BALL—SQUAT AND PULL

a

b

Purpose: To develop dynamic strength for performing turnovers during rugby play.

Procedure

1. Squat down and firmly grip with one or both hands a dumbbell or a double-grip medicine ball on the floor.

2. Using both your arms and your legs to generate the backward movement, explosively pull the dumbbell or medicine ball from the floor, twist, and jump back, as if you are ripping a ball from an opponent. Slowly return the dumbbell or medicine ball to the floor and assume the start position.

3. Do four repetitions with the same arm, then four more with the other arm, pulling and twisting in the other direction. This equals one set. Perform two to four sets, with four minutes' rest between sets.

Key point: Select a load that you can move quickly, such as an 8- to 10-kilogram medicine ball or dumbbell.

STEP AND HAND OFF

Purpose: To develop dynamic strength for performing a hand-off to an opponent.

Procedure

1. Stand upright with the handle of a cable pulley device or weighted sled positioned at chest height in your right hand.

2. Using your right hand and leg to generate the movement, explosively lunge and aggressively push the handle forward, as if you are handing off a player at chest height. Apply maximum speed during the drill. Slowly return to the start position with the load and repeat with the left arm and leg.

3. Do four repetitions on each side, rest for four minutes, then repeat for four sets.

Key point: Select a level of resistance that can be moved quickly but requires great effort, such as 30 percent of your body weight.

PARTNER WRESTLE

a

Purpose: To develop dynamic strength for tackling, wrestling, and mauling.

Procedure

1. Stand facing a partner. Hold a strength bar or ash pole between you, alternating your hands (one player's right hand, then the other player's left hand, then the first player's left hand, then the second player's right hand, as shown in figure a). A variation of this is to have the players grasp either end of the bar (figure b).

b

2. With your knees slightly bent, hollow and brace your abdomen and react to your coach's order to pull or push. Exert the maximum effort to try to make your partner move.

Key point: Use your whole body to generate the pushing and pulling, not just your arms.

DRIVING MAUL

Purpose: To develop dynamic strength for driving mauls. The pushing movement in this group drill (for two to four players) also loads the triple-extension movement, which enhances explosive power.

Equipment and area: An automobile (engine switched off) and a firm, grassy area.

Procedure

1. Stand with the group at the rear of an automobile.

2. Instruct the driver to release the parking break. Explosively push the car for 10 to 15 seconds, focusing on leaning your body forward and taking fast and short steps. Exert maximum effort while pushing.

3. Allow four minutes for recovery between four to eight tries.

Key point: Vary the group's position behind the car to one side or in the middle.

SAMPLE STRENGTH AND POWER TRAINING PROGRAMS

These programs isolate specific elements of strength and power, including core stabilization, pattern strength, and loaded strength and power.

Six-Week Core Stabilization Program

Aims: To improve the recruitment and endurance of the key stabilizers of the trunk, including the abdominal, gluteal, lower-back, shoulder, and neck muscles

Guidelines

- Perform three to four sessions per week, alternating between sessions 1 and 2.

- Progress by adding an extra set of each drill during weeks 4 through 6.

SESSION 1

Drill	Sets	Repetitions × duration (s.)	Rest between sets
Abdominal Hollow and Brace	3	5 × 5	30 s.
Bent Knee to Sky	3	15	30 s.
Deep Neck	3	5 × 5	30 s.
Arm and Leg Raise	3	5 × 5 (each side)	45 s.
Single-Leg Bridge	3	5 × 5	45 s.
T Raises	3	10	45 s.

SESSION 2

Drill	Sets	Repetitions × duration (s.)	Rest between sets
Leg Raise and Support	3	10	30 s.
Rotating Ramp	3	3 (each position)	45 s.
Prone Extensions	3	15	60 s.
Shoulder Step-Up	3	8	60 s.
Squat and Squeeze	3	5 × 5	60 s.
Swiss Ball Maul	3	3 × 10	30 s.

Six-Week Pattern Strength Program

Aims: To improve functional strength and simulate many of the movements of rugby, such as lunging, twisting, and squatting. This program also integrates dynamic core stabilization and control drills.

Guidelines

- Perform three to four sessions per week, alternating between sessions 1 and 2.

- For the drills marked with *, introduce a load such as a 5- to 10-kg weighted vest or use a 3- to 5-kg medicine ball during weeks 3 and 4 and increase to a 10- to 15-kg vest or 5- to 10-kg medicine ball during weeks 5 and 6.

- Progress by adding an extra set of each drill during weeks 4 through 6.

SESSION 1

Drill	Sets	Repetitions × duration (s.)	Rest between sets
Squat and Squeeze	2	5 × 5	45 s.
Lunge and Dummy Pass	4	10	45 s.
Swiss Ball Maul	5	1 × 10	20 s.
Push-Up and Pull	3	6	60 s.
Multidirectional Lunge*	3	6	90 s.
Shoulder Step-Up	3	10	90 s.
Lateral Wall Squat*	3	8	90 s.

SESSION 2 Drill	Sets	Repetitions × duration (s.)	Rest between sets
Reach and Touch Down	4	10	60 s.
Supine Maul-Up	3	6	90 s.
Single-Leg Squat and Dummy Pass	3	10	90 s.
Neck Stabilizer	3	3 × 10	
Multichop	3	5 (each side)	60 s.

Nine-Week Loaded Strength Program

Aims: To develop general and maximum strength.

Guidelines

- Perform two to three sessions per week, alternating between sessions 1 and 2.

- Ensure that you have at least one day between loaded strength sessions.

- When selecting loads, ensure that you are able to complete the designated set of repetitions by lifting to fatigue and not to failure.

- For the drills marked with *, progress by increasing the load by 5 to 10 percent every three weeks and reduce the repetitions by 2 (for example, on weeks 4 through 6 perform 8 repetitions, on weeks 7 through 9 perform 6 repetitions). Continue this theme until you are performing sets of 4 repetitions.

- Increase your rest between sets by 30 seconds when you reduce the sets by 2 repetitions (for example, at week 7, the Back Squat will be 3 × 6 repetitions with 2:30 minutes rest.

SESSION 1

Drill	Sets	Repetitions × duration (s.)	Rest between sets
Back Squat*	3	10	90 s.
Hamstring Pendulum	3	10	90 s.
Bent-Over Row*	3	10	90 s.
Shoulder Press*	3	10	90 s.
Front and Lateral Raises	3	10	90 s.

SESSION 2

Drill	Sets	Repetitions × duration (s.)	Rest between sets
Front Squat*	3	10	90 s.
Single-Leg Deadlift with no dummy pass (see Single-Leg Squat and Dummy Pass for guidelines)	3	10 (each leg)	90 s.
Weighted Push-Up*	3	10	90 s.
Bench Press*	3	10	90 s.
T Raises (with light dumbbells)	3	10	90 s.

Nine-Week Power Program

Aims: To develop power (speed strength). All of these drills should be performed explosively with control.

Guidelines

- Perform two to three sessions per week, alternating between sessions 1 and 2.

- Ensure that you have at least one day between power sessions and that you are fresh when starting these sessions.

- Begin the program with a light load—a load that you would be able to lift for 9 repetitions (9RM load). The light load allows you to move the bar quickly.

- For the drills marked with *, progress by increasing the load by 10 to 15 percent every three weeks—for example, weeks 1 to 3 light load (9RM), weeks 4 to 6 medium load (7RM), weeks 7 to 9 heavy load (5RM).
- Start with 5RM load for the Bench Press, assuming that you have completed a loaded strength program similar to the program listed previously.

SESSION 1

Drill	Sets	Repetitions	Superset	Rest between sets
Power Pull*	4	4	1 × Catch, Release, Drop, and Go!	4 min.
Hang Snatch*	3	4	Jump and Fix × 1	4 min.
Turnover Ball— Squat and Pull	4	6		4 min.

SESSION 2

Drill	Sets	Repetitions	Comment	Rest between sets
Power Clean*	3	4	This drill is a Power-Up before moving outside for Tackle Breaker!	4 min.
Tackle Breaker!	6	2	Repetition 1 with sled/vest, repetition 2 without, 60 s. between reps.	4 min.
Step and Hand Off	4	4	Using sled, perform 4 reps on each arm/ leg.	4 min.

CHAPTER 7

SPEED AND AGILITY DRILLS

Speed and agility—the keys to winning at rugby—are enviable abilities that have helped Dan to score over 30 tries as an international player. They allow players to accelerate and reach top speeds from varying starting positions, to sustain top speeds in open field space, and to avoid defenders by quickly changing direction while maintaining the pace. Being able to decelerate and stop rapidly under control are also crucial, both in attack and defense.

To have speed is to have the ability to produce a movement in the quickest possible time, whereas *agility* refers to the way in which speed is applied in rugby, encompassing starting and stopping movement as well as changing direction swiftly and with control. These elements can be learned in isolation, but ultimately, rugby-specific speed and agility are gained in drills that combine and challenge both qualities and mimic the movement patterns experienced in games.

Speed for rugby players is different from the speed demonstrated by top track sprinters. The time taken to reach top speed, the running posture, and the arm actions are all different. Track athletes hit their top speed about 65 to 75 meters into a 100-meter race, whereas rugby players reach peak speed much sooner and cover shorter distances. Rugby players rarely sprint more than 30 meters, and the majority of breaks and chases in rugby are of less than 10 meters, which shows why acceleration is the major speed element to develop.

The ideal running posture for rugby players is also specific to the sport. Rugby players tend to run with a closed upper-body posture and a notable forward lean, as opposed to track athletes, who run tall with an open chest. Running lower and in a more compact posture reduces exposure to tacklers while also enhancing body position, deceleration, and turning to make tackles or hit rucks. When players are in open field space, they should use track running form to improve running efficiency and maintain basic speed. *Basic speed* is the term used to describe sprinting following the acceleration phase.

HOW ARE RUGBY SPEED AND AGILITY DEVELOPED?

Some people are naturally fast and others excel at running long distances, but most people fall somewhere in between. Most international players, particularly outside backs, are naturally fast, and this quality is refined with speed and agility training, particularly acceleration and foot-speed drills that are vital to performance over short distances and in multidirectional running. In comparison, elite front-row forwards are naturally big, strong, and powerful, qualities that help them to generate speed from various starting positions, such as from the ground, off a scrum, and through defenders.

Strength and power drills, particularly explosive lifting, medicine ball, and plyometric drills, improve a player's speed and agility development. These drills simulate the triple extension of the ankle, knee, and hip joints that occurs during the acceleration phase of sprinting and helps players to develop the rapid force required for initiating movement and changing direction. Players with high levels of strength and power are more likely to have high levels of speed and agility. See chapter 6 for drills and more information about strength and power.

BENEFITS OF SPEED AND AGILITY DRILLS

Speed and agility training, an integral part of training for all top players, can help players evade tacklers, catch attackers, retreat according to referees' commands, avoid injury, perform lineout movements, and catch passes.

> ## Dan's Top Tip

One mistake I made early in my career was to concentrate too much on general speed and power in my training at the expense of rugby-specific movements. Rugby players can benefit by learning the techniques of competitors in pure performance disciplines like track and field, but only if they are applied to physical situations that occur on a rugby pitch. You can be the fastest on the team, but if you can't change direction, drop your shoulder, and shift your weight for a tackle, then your speed becomes a weakness rather than a strength.

POSITION-SPECIFIC SPEED AND AGILITY

Forwards, who perform the majority of sprints over distances of three to eight meters, focus on taking short strides to enable them to quickly change direction in response to the chaotic nature of forward play. A lineout jumper, for example, requires agility to quickly step forward and backward to lose an opponent prior to jumping for the ball. In comparison, a wing or fullback has the luxury of having more time to generate speed from a rolling start when he or she enters the line during the attack or counterattack on receiving a deep kick. Most speed and agility drills in this chapter are relevant for all positions, but positional and skill-specific drills are also included.

MECHANICS OF SPEED

Speed can be broken down into acceleration and basic speed. Rugby relies heavily on acceleration speed (the ability to rapidly reach high speeds from various starting positions), but it also requires basic speed (the ability to maintain peak velocity) which has its own mechanical rules. The mechanics of acceleration and basic speed provide a framework for optimizing technique when performing these movements.

Acceleration and Deceleration Mechanics

During the early phase of acceleration, the emphasis is on extending the ankles, knees, and hips in a triple extension. A forward lean is required to generate momentum and a straight line may be drawn from the heel to the head to represent the optimum running posture. The rapid and synchronized arm action, led by the shoulders, generates the stride rate while counteracting the rotational force produced by the legs. Runners should have a sense of pushing off the balls of their feet.

Optimal deceleration mechanics require rapidly reducing momentum with multiple short steps while maintaining the center of gravity over or in front of the knees, especially when slowing from a sprint at near-maximal or maximal speeds. This fast foot action also allows players to reaccelerate. Staying upright and using large steps to slow down places high forces on the major knee ligaments and should be avoided.

Strength drills such as lunges and squats develop the muscles responsible for stabilizing the knee joint during deceleration and help absorb the forces placed on the ligaments.

High knee lifting should not be used in either acceleration or deceleration because it increases the time between foot strikes.

Basic Speed Mechanics

Posture during the basic speed phase of sprinting is more upright and, like posture during acceleration, a straight line can be drawn from the ankle of the supporting leg through the knee, hip, trunk, and head. Lifting the knees higher increases stride length and should be encouraged. Key basic speed principles include

1. relax your face, shoulders, and hands;
2. ensure that your feet land under or slightly behind your hips and that you lift your knees higher than you do during acceleration, bringing your thighs almost parallel with the ground;
3. move your arms with a smooth forward-backward action—not across your body—driving backward with your elbows and moving your hands between shoulder and hip height; and
4. keep your elbows at a 90-degree angle between your upper and lower arms.

The goal during basic speed performance is to have a fluid running motion similar to that of a track sprinter.

MECHANICS OF AGILITY

That players generate speed from varying starting positions and change direction quickly without decreasing speed are two reasons that rugby is such an exciting and evasive sport. These movements require the player to shift the body's center of gravity and control the movement by using foot speed, balance, and fast reactions. Players should focus on staying low to the ground while taking short steps and planting their feet at various angles to generate directional changes.

Balance is a fundamental component of agility. When you move forward or change direction, the stabilizing muscles have to react and control the movement because the trunk provides the foundation for the dynamic movement of the arms and legs. Poor balance, regardless of the levels of leg strength and power, will result in poor mechanics, a reduction in speed production, and possibly injury.

Because rugby is a multidirectional sport, foot speed is vital for effective and efficient positioning, particularly on the advantage line. Whether you make a tackle or avoid a defender depends on your foot speed. Reducing the time between foot strikes lets you change speed and direction more quickly.

Dan's Top Tip

I try to concentrate on keeping my legs (and therefore the propulsive power) underneath me. In other words, do not reach for a longer stride or take a huge sidestep, because they will only slow you down. Concentrate on making fast movements with your body in balance, retaining speed and momentum. Track athletes talk about "running in a box"—retaining a controlled, powerful, and efficient running style—and I try to do that rather than letting my form fall apart with too much exaggerated effort.

EFFECT OF BALL CARRYING

Carrying a ball in one or both hands reduces the effectiveness of the arm action that promotes stride rate and balance and places more stress on the core stabilizing muscles. Performing the dynamic core stabilization drills in chapter 6 will therefore improve those mechanics.

Players should practice speed and agility drills both with and without a ball and try to minimize the disruption that carrying the ball causes in running mechanics. Switch between carrying the ball in one and both hands to simulate situations in rugby play. Also bear in mind that during 80 minutes of rugby, the average player rarely has the ball in his or her hand for a total of more than 45 seconds.

INJURY PREVENTION AND RECONDITIONING

Most noncontact lower-body injuries in rugby occur during speed and agility movements. These activities, particularly changing direction quickly or when fatigued, place great demands on the muscles and joints. By practicing a progressive range of speed and agility drills, your chance of sustaining injury during these movements is significantly reduced. In addition, your training program must also include control, pattern, and loaded strength drills.

After prolonged inactivity caused by an injury, speed and agility training must be introduced in accordance with three underlying principles:

- Ensure that sufficient levels of strength and stability have returned to the injured body part.
- Ensure that the range of motion in the injured area has returned to normal.
- Gradually progress from programmed to reactive speed and agility drills.

Players should not return to full rugby training or competition until they have completed a speed and agility program and are able to sprint maximally with changes in direction. Always consult your physician or physiotherapist when you suffer an injury and during rehabilitation and retraining.

DRILLS FOR SPEED AND AGILITY

Speed drills are separated into technique, acceleration, deceleration, and basic speed drills. Acceleration drills also include lateral and backward acceleration movements. Agility drills are either programmed or reactive and combine acceleration, deceleration, and multidirectional running from varying starting positions. In programmed drills, the player knows the movement combinations and sequence, but in reactive drills, the player must react to a stimulus such as a ball, defender, attacker, or instructions from a coach. Reactive drills are more rugby-specific, whereas programmed drills isolate and rehearse certain movement patterns.

Developing agility and speed is a neuromuscular process. Improvement comes when muscles remember movements and perform them with increased speed, efficiency, and control. Certain training principles facilitate progress:

- Sessions should be short in duration.
- Recovery between drills should be maximal.
- Players should not start a speed or agility drill when they are fatigued.
- Players must perform a thorough warm-up before speed and agility drills. Refer to chapter 4 for guidelines.
- Players should use foot speed, balance, and programmed agility drills before introducing reactive agility drills.
- Players can progress to holding a ball during drills if it is appropriate.
- Players must learn to relax their face, neck, arms, and shoulders during all drills.

Perform new drills slowly and then gradually increase your foot speed, acceleration, and deceleration. Because these drills challenge the nervous system, they should not be performed more than two or three times per week, and for no more than 45 minutes.

TECHNIQUE DRILLS

These drills help develop the mechanics necessary for effective rugby speed and agility. They may be used in isolation or as part of a warm-up.

FORWARD AND LATERAL SKIPPING

Purpose: To develop fast feet and rapid ground reaction force. This drill encourages you to flex and extend your feet, forces your feet to move fast, and highlights the notion of a dynamic foot strike.

Procedure

1. Skip (alternating hops and steps) forward over a distance of 20 to 30 meters. Focus on pushing off the ball of the foot and gradually increase the distance between skips by pushing off the ground harder and faster. Lean forward slightly and aggressively drive your arms to support the skips.

2. Rest as you walk back to the start position.

3. Skip laterally over the same distance, focusing on pushing off the trailing leg. Keep your hands up to maintain your balance.

4. Perform two repetitions of forward and lateral skipping with a walk-back recovery. Rest for two to three minutes and repeat for three sets.

Progression

- Gradually increase the distance between skips.

- Hug a ball to your chest.

BACKWARD RUNNING

Purpose: To develop fast and efficient backward-movement mechanics. Backward running should be done with short, sidelong skipping steps at a 45-degree angle so that players can maintain better balance and control, allowing them to quickly change direction.

Procedure

1. Set your hips and feet at a 45-degree angle to the direction that you are facing. Run backward for 10 meters, focusing on pushing backward with the balls of both feet, minimizing ground contact time.

2. Change direction sharply after each 10-meter run.

3. Perform three repetitions, walking back to the start position for recovery. Do three sets, allowing three minutes' rest between sets.

Key points

- Minimize knee lift to increase your stride rate.

- Keep your arms close to your body with your elbows flexed to help you maintain your balance.

- Lean your body slightly forward so that your center of gravity is above or in front of your planting knee.

Progression: Quickly change from backward to forward running. The backward running mechanics emphasized in this drill help players to quickly change direction while running.

BODY LEAN ACCELERATIONS

Purpose: To develop the proper posture and body lean for effective acceleration.

Equipment and area: Flat surface.

Procedure

1. Stand facing a partner. Adopt a pronounced forward lean while your partner supports you by holding your shoulders.
2. When your partner stops supporting you and moves to the side, immediately accelerate forward from the overbalanced position to run five meters.
3. Gradually slow down and return to the start position. Rest for 30 seconds.
4. Each partner should perform six repetitions.

Key points

- When accelerating, keep the ball of your foot behind your hips and dynamically impact the ground, pushing it away from your body.
- Drive your arms rapidly, punching the elbows backward and maintaining a 90-degree angle at the elbow.

ACCELERATION DRILLS

Acceleration drills focus on distances of between 5 and 25 meters. The objective is to cover the distance as quickly as possible while still adhering to the correct acceleration mechanics.

HOLLOW SPRINTS

Purpose: To improve acceleration and the ability to rapidly change running speed.

Equipment and area: Seven cones, sixty-meter-long track or flat surface.

Procedure: Position a cone at 5 meters, 10 meters, 20 meters, 30 meters, 45 meters, and 60 meters from a start line.

1. Jog to the first cone, sprint to the second cone, jog to the third cone, sprint to the fourth cone, jog to the fifth cone, and then sprint to the sixth cone.

2. Rest for three minutes, then repeat for six run-throughs.

Key points

- As you approach a sprint cone, begin to lean forward to accelerate.
- Apply correct deceleration mechanics as you slow down to jogging speed between cones.

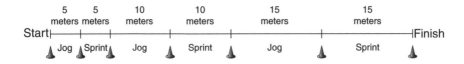

MEDICINE BALL CHUCK AND CHASE

Purpose: To develop forward and lateral acceleration by using an overspeed effect. The momentum generated by passing the ball increases speed off the mark.

Equipment and area: Grassy area of a minimum of 10 by 30 meters and a medicine ball (three to five kilograms).

Procedure

1. From a standing position, explosively bend your hips and knees and, from chest level, chuck a medicine ball as far as possible. This will give your posture a forward lean.

2. Immediately accelerate after the ball.

3. Run past the medicine ball before it stops rolling then gradually slow down.

4. Alternatively, explosively throw the medicine ball across your body and chase it down so that you start accelerating from a rotational position. First, swing the ball to the right, then to the left, release, and follow the ball, aiming to run past the ball before it stops rolling.

5. Allow time for a full recovery (about two minutes) between each of six repetitions.

Key points

- Aim for distance, not height, when chucking the ball.
- The overspeed effect of chucking the ball makes your acceleration more explosive.
- Push off from the balls of your feet when you release the ball.

Progression: Perform the drill on a slight downhill to increase the overspeed effect.

RESISTED ACCELERATION DRILLS

Resisted running drills are a recognized method of developing acceleration speed. A form of speed strength training, they use resistance (as a load or gradient) to overload the muscles responsible for acceleration speed. There are three types of resisted running drills:

1. Resisted sled or chute drills develop acceleration by supplying horizontal resistance to the pushing movement of the driving leg. The recommended sled load is 10 percent of body weight.

2. Weighted vest drills challenge the player with vertical resistance by loading the legs when they strike the floor and develop reactive speed strength for improved acceleration. The recommended load is 10 percent of body weight.

3. Hill or stair drills use gravity to create the resistance as the player climbs.

Resisted acceleration sessions must include sprints with no resistance to allow the body to benefit from unrestricted movement and maximize muscle excitation. It is also important to progress to performing these drills with slight changes in direction and backward and lateral movement to prepare players for the multidirectional nature of rugby. Use a lighter load (5 to 10 percent of body weight) during these drills.

SLED ACCELERATIONS

Purpose: To develop acceleration using horizontal resistance.

Equipment and area: Track or grassy area of a minimum of 30 meters in length, and a sled loaded with a weight not exceeding 10 percent of body weight.

Procedure

1. Attach the harness and crouch with your back to the front of a stopped sled, then accelerate and pull the sled straight ahead for 20 meters.

2. Rest for 3 minutes, then return to the start position and repeat two more times. Then perform a 20-meter sprint with no resistance. Do two of these sets.

3. Lateral resistance. Grip the harness or a handle attached to the sled with your hand (as opposed to attaching a harness). From a crouched start position, grip the handle with your right hand, then accelerate sideways and pull the sled 10 meters to your left, rest for 1 minute, grip the handle with your left hand, and then accelerate and pull the sled back to the start position.

4. Rest for 3 minutes, then repeat for three sets.

5. After the third set, do two sets of sprinting 10 meters sideways to the left, resting for 1 minute, and sideways back to the start position.

6. Backward resistance. Crouch facing the loaded sled and set your hips and feet at a 45-degree angle to the direction that you are facing. Gripping its handle with one hand, accelerate and pull the sled for 10 meters, rest for 30 seconds, then repeat with the other

hand. Rest for 3 minutes, then repeat with no resistance. Repeat for a total of three sets.

Key points

- Focus on a dynamic foot strike and arm action.
- Focus on keeping a low body position with forward lean for maximum power generation.
- For the lateral and backward resisted running drills, reduce the resistance to 5 to 7.5 percent of body weight. Adhere to the mechanics of lateral and backward running as detailed in the Technique Drills section.

STADIUM STEP ACCELERATIONS

Purpose: To develop acceleration using resistance.

Equipment and area: Stadium steps and a stopwatch.

Procedure

1. Sprint up approximately 30 stadium steps by using the quickest method (usually 2 steps at a time, depending on player height and step depth). Focus on the triple extension of the ankles, knees, and hips, and drive your arms vigorously.

2. Record the time it takes to reach the top step, then walk back down to the start position, resting for two to three minutes.

3. Repeat for six to eight sprints, or until it takes 15 percent longer to perform.

Progression

- Use the stadium steps for a foot-speed drill, running up every step instead of every other one.
- Run up every step laterally to improve lateral foot speed.

WEIGHTED VEST ACCELERATIONS

Purpose: To develop acceleration using vertical resistance.

Equipment and area: Track or grassy area of at least 30 meters long and a weighted vest weighing no more than 10 percent of body weight.

Procedure

1. Drill 1. Wearing the vest, crouch at the start position and accelerate forward for 20 meters. Rest for three minutes and repeat. Rest for two minutes after the second repetition and then repeat without the vest. Rest for four minutes.

2. Drill 2. Wearing the vest, lie facedown on the ground. On command, get up as quickly as possible, focusing on staying low, and sprint 10 meters. Rest for two minutes and repeat. Rest for two minutes after the second repetition and then repeat without the vest. Rest for four minutes.

3. Drill 3. Wearing the vest, lie facedown on the ground. On command, roll to the side 360 degrees, get up, and sprint 10 meters. Rest for two minutes and repeat. Rest for two minutes after the second repetition and then repeat without the vest. Rest for four minutes.

4. Drill 4. Wearing the vest, crouch at the start position, then accelerate forward for 10 meters, turn to face the opposite direction, run backward for 10 meters, drop to the ground and get up as quickly as possible, and sprint the 20 meters back to the start line. Rest for three minutes and repeat. Rest for two minutes after the second repetition and then repeat without the vest. Rest for four minutes.

5. Drill 5. For a lateral resisted running drill, wear the vest as you skip laterally (see Lateral Skipping guidelines under Technique Drills earlier in this chapter) to the left for 10 meters, then immediately skip laterally to the right for 10 meters. Rest for two minutes and repeat. Rest for two minutes after the second repetition and then repeat without the vest. Rest for four minutes.

Key point: Do only three of the five drills in one session.

DECELERATION DRILLS

Deceleration drills challenge and develop a player's ability to stop quickly. Although most players include acceleration drills in their training program, deceleration drills are equally important. The goal with each drill is to slow down quickly by applying the correct deceleration mechanics.

Drills in the agility section of this chapter also develop deceleration speed.

GRADED DECELERATIONS

Purpose: To develop deceleration at various running speeds.

Equipment and area: Grassy area of a minimum of 10 by 30 meters and a whistle.

Procedure: This drill is split into four progressions. The player is to stop effectively in response to the coach's whistle.

1. Drill 1. The player runs at half of his or her maximum speed. After 10 to 15 meters, the coach blows the whistle. The player tries to stop within three short steps. The player rests for one minute, then repeats for at least three repetitions before progressing to drill 2.

2. Drill 2. The player runs at three-quarters of maximum speed. After 10 to 15 meters, the coach blows the whistle. The player tries to stop within five short steps. The player rests for two minutes, then repeats for at least three repetitions before progressing to drill 3.

3. Drill 3. The player runs at full speed. After 15 to 25 meters, the coach blows the whistle. The player tries to stop within seven short steps. The player rests for two minutes, then repeats for at least three repetitions before progressing to drill 4.

4. Drill 4. The player runs at full speed. After 15 to 25 meters, the coach blows the whistle. The player tries to stop within seven short steps and then immediately accelerates for 5 meters. The player rests for three minutes, then repeats for three repetitions.

Key point: Focus on taking short steps with your body weight over or in front of your knees.

Progression: Players who exhibit high levels of leg strength can progress to wearing a weighted vest (with 10 percent of body weight) during these drills.

BASIC SPEED DRILLS

Basic speed refers to sprinting after the acceleration phase of running, and these drills develop speed for open field running. The mechanics of basic speed favor an upright posture.

ROLL AND RUN

Purpose: To develop basic speed.

Equipment and area: Track or grassy area of a minimum of 100 meters in length and five cones.

Procedure: Position the cones 20 meters apart. The drill is split into three progressions.

1. Drill 1. From a standing start at cone 1, accelerate to three-quarters of maximum speed to cone 2. On reaching cone 2, explode with your arms and increase your knee-lift height to adopt a basic speed running style. Run at maximum speed to cone 3. Rest for three minutes and repeat, but accelerate at maximum speed to cone 2 before adopting the basic speed technique to run to cone 3. Rest for four minutes.

2. Drill 2. Repeat drill 1, accelerating at three-quarters of maximum speed to cone 2 and then adopting the basic speed technique to run at maximum speed to cone 4. Rest for three minutes, then repeat, but with maximum acceleration between cones 1 and 2. Rest for four minutes.

3. Drill 3. Repeat drill 1, accelerating at three-quarters of maximum speed to cone 3 and then adopting the basic speed technique to run at maximum speed to cone 5. Rest for three minutes, then repeat, but with maximum acceleration between cones 1 and 3. Rest for four minutes.

Key points

- Focus on technique more than running speed. Although the basic speed phase should be completed at or at close to maximum speed, do not sacrifice form for speed.
- Do not overreach (take extra-long strides to gain extra ground).

Progression: Perform the drills on a slight downhill gradient of 3 to 5 percent to create an overspeed feeling with help from the gradient.

Dan's Top Tip

Use a hill with a slight downhill gradient for good overspeed training to encourage players to increase their stride length and knee lift.

AGILITY DRILLS

Agility training is divided between balance and foot-speed drills, which develop the two fundamental components of effective rugby agility. Programmed and reactive drills integrate these qualities with acceleration and deceleration to develop specific, multidirectional rugby movement patterns.

1. **Balance drills.** Balance is a fundamental quality that relies on the stabilizing and proprioceptive properties of muscles to maintain control. Balance drills also help to prevent knee and ankle injuries. Several of these drills are performed with the eyes closed so the body has to rely solely on feedback from the muscles and joints. Balance also depends on core stability and functional leg strength. These elements are covered in chapter 6.

2. **Foot-speed drills.** *Foot speed* is the ability to quickly touch the foot to the ground and remove it. The speed at which the feet can move is dictated by how efficiently the joints of the lower body work together with support from the trunk and arm drive. Ladder, box, and skipping drills force the legs and feet to adapt to the spaces between the rungs, lines, and skip steps to encourage fast patterns of footwork.

3. **Programmed agility drills.** These drills deal with various rugby movement patterns that require agility, such as quickly changing between forward, backward, and lateral running; sidestepping or swerving past defenders; and avoiding an opponent during a lineout jump. When performing programmed drills, the player knows the sequence of events and movement combinations.

4. **Reactive agility drills.** In reactive drills, the player must react to a stimulus such as a ball, defender, attacker, or instructions from a coach. These drills incorporate a multitude of movements that players must use during competition.

BALANCE DRILLS

Following are two balance drills to help maintain muscle control and prevent knee and ankle injuries.

EYES WIDE SHUT

Purpose: To develop balance. This series of drills develops awareness and control, qualities that prevent injury and enhance agility.

Procedure: The aim of each drill is to stabilize yourself on one leg with your eyes shut. Avoid swaying from side to side, and focus on fixing your foot to the floor and holding firm.

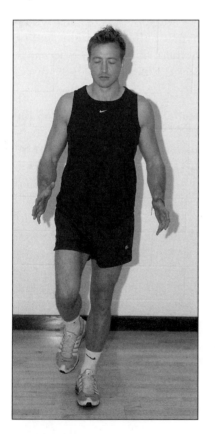

1. Drill 1. Stand on one leg on flat ground and close both of your eyes for 15 seconds. Try to stand perfectly still. Open your eyes and then repeat with the other leg. Do four repetitions, then rest for 10 seconds.

2. Drill 2. Repeat drill 1 while also waving your arms about randomly to increase the challenge. Do four repetitions, then rest for 10 seconds.

3. Drill 3. Lie face down on flat ground with your eyes shut. On command, stand up and balance on one leg as fast as possible while keeping your eyes shut for 10 seconds. Repeat with the other leg. Do four repetitions, then rest for 10 seconds.

4. Drill 4. With your eyes closed, perform a double-leg jump, but land on one leg. Repeat with the other leg. Do four repetitions. Do not do drill 4 if you cannot successfully do drills 1 through 3.

Progression: Have a partner challenge your balance by randomly pushing and pulling you as you balance on one leg with your eyes closed.

REACH FOR BALANCE!

Purpose: To develop balance in multiple planes of movement. There is a high strength element to this progressive set of single-leg drills.

Equipment and area: Flat ground and five tall cones (maximum height 20 centimeters).

Procedure: The aim of the drill is to reach for and touch each of the five cones as you balance on one leg. Position two of the cones half a meter apart with two other cones one meter across from the first two and half a meter from each other. Position the center cone one meter from where the player stands and midway between the two rows of two cones.

1. Drill 1. Balance on your right leg, then squat low and reach to your right with your right hand and touch the cone there. Return to the start position and repeat the drill, but reach to the left with your left

hand and touch the cone there. Do five repetitions, then change legs and repeat. Rest for two minutes.

2. Drill 2. Repeat drill 1, but touch the cone to your left with your right hand and the cone to your right with your left hand. Do five repetitions, then change legs and repeat. Rest for two minutes.

3. Drill 3. Repeat drill 1, but touch the cones with both hands simultaneously. Do five repetitions, then change legs and repeat. Rest for two minutes.

4. Drill 4. Balance on your right leg, then squat low and reach forward to touch the center cone with first your right hand, then both hands, and then your left hand. Return to the start position and do three repetitions, then change legs and repeat. Rest for two minutes.

5. Drill 5. Repeat as above, but touch the diagonal cones with first the right, then the left, and then both hands. Do five repetitions, then change legs and repeat.

Key points

- These drills are progressive and should not be performed out of sequence.

- Move on to the next drill only if you successfully performed the previous drill.

FOOT-SPEED DRILLS

Foot-speed drills include ladder drills and skipping rope (jump rope). They are ideal warm-up routines.

Skipping is a great athleticism drill because it challenges hand-eye and hand-foot coordination and develops foot speed and balance. Skipping is also fun and a perfect way to start plyometric or speed and agility drills.

TOP-FIVE LADDER DRILLS

Purpose: To develop foot speed with a progressive series of ladder drills. The length of the ladder permits players to repeat movements so they learn them quickly and effectively, and the rungs can be manipulated to suit a variety of drills.

Equipment and area: Flat ground and a foot-speed ladder (with a minimum of eight rungs).

Procedure: The goal of each drill is to minimize your knee lift and move your feet through the ladder as quickly as possible. Start each drill at a comfortable pace and gradually increase your foot speed while you move your arms in sequence with your legs. Lean forward and close your upper-body posture, in accordance with acceleration running mechanics, as you perform these drills, and vigorously pump your arms to increase your foot speed.

1. Drill 1. One foot each square. Stand on both feet in front of a foot-speed ladder that is lying on the ground. Run the length of the ladder by placing one foot in each ladder space. See figure a. Do four repetitions, with a walk-back recovery between each repetition. Then rest for two minutes.

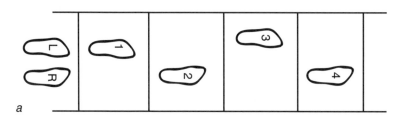

a

2. Drill 2. Two feet each square. Stand on both feet in front of the ladder. Run the length of the ladder by placing both feet in each ladder space. See figure b. Do four repetitions, with a walk-back recovery between each repetition. Then rest for two minutes.

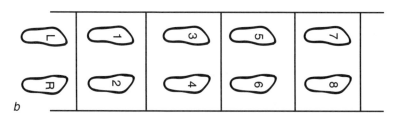

b

3. Drill 3. Two feet each square laterally. Stand on both feet sideways in front of the ladder. Run the length of the ladder by moving laterally through it, placing both feet in each space. See figure c. Walk back to the start position and repeat, facing in the opposite direction and leading with the other leg. Do four repetitions, with a walk-back recovery between each repetition. Then rest for two minutes.

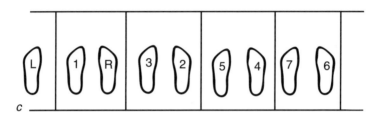

c

4. Drill 4. Two in, two out. Stand on both feet sideways in the first ladder space. Move laterally down the ladder, leading with the nearest foot, and place two feet behind the first space (so you are stepping backward out of the ladder), then two feet into the next space. Repeat this sequence along the length of the ladder. See figure d. Walk back to the start position and repeat, facing in the opposite direction and leading with the other leg. Do four repetitions, with a walk-back recovery between each repetition. Then rest for two minutes.

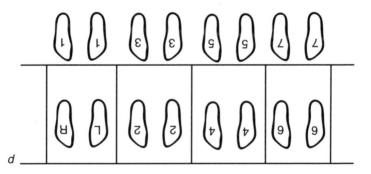

d

5. Drill 5. Side step. Sidestep into and out of each space as you move forward. The pattern is, for example, to move the left foot into the first ladder space, move the right foot into the same space, move the left foot outside the ladder, move the right foot into the second ladder space, move the left foot into the same space, and move the

right foot outside the ladder. Mentally counting one-two-out, one-two-out, and so on will help you capture the rhythm. Gradually increase how far outside the ladder you step as you move down the ladder. See figure e. Do four repetitions, with a walk-back recovery between each repetition. Then rest for two minutes.

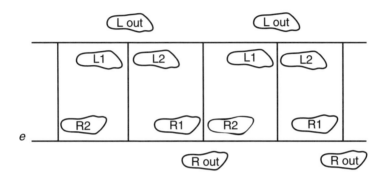

e

Key points

- These drills are progressive and should not be performed out of sequence.
- Move on to the next drill only if you successfully performed the previous drill.

SKIPPING MEDLEY

Purpose: To develop foot speed, coordination, and balance with a series of drills.

Equipment and area: Flat ground, skipping rope, and a stopwatch.

Procedure: When skipping rope, rotate the rope rapidly as you quickly move your feet and maintain a stable trunk. Jump just high enough to clear the rope, landing on the balls of your feet. Slightly bend your knees during all movement patterns and minimize your arm movement. Gradually increase the skipping speed as your technique improves.

1. Drill 1. Double-leg skip. Perform a double-leg jump between each rope turn for 20 seconds, then rest for 1 minute. Do three repetitions.

2. Drill 2. Alternate-leg stride skips. Alternate between left- and right-foot skips for 20 seconds, then rest for 1 minute. Do three repetitions.

3. Drill 3. Heel-toe. Bounce once between each rope turn, alternating so that the heel of one foot and the toe of the opposite foot make contact with the ground at the same time. Skip for 20 seconds, then rest for 1 minute. Do three repetitions.

4. Drill 4. Lateral double-leg skips. Keeping your legs together, skip first to one side and then to the other during the next rope turn. Skip for 20 seconds, then rest for 1 minute. Do three repetitions.

5. Drill 5. Lateral single-leg skips. Repeat drill 4, but skip using only one leg for 10 seconds, and then switch to the other leg for 10 seconds. Skip for 20 seconds, then rest for 1 minute. Do three repetitions.

Progression

- These drills are progressive and should not be performed out of sequence.

- Move on to the next drill only if you successfully performed the previous drill.

- Use a skipping rope with a counter to monitor the maximum number of skips you perform in 1 minute.

- Start a skipping league and compare the 1-minute skipping performance of team members.

PROGRAMMED SPEED AND AGILITY DRILLS

Programmed drills combine foot speed, balance, acceleration, deceleration, and changes in direction to form rugby-specific movement drills.

BAG DRILL

Purpose: To develop forward, lateral, and backward running speed and agility.

Equipment and area: Grassy area of a minimum of 10 by 30 meters and four to six tackle bags.

Procedure

1. Position four tackle bags 3 meters apart.

2. Moving as quickly as possible, accelerate forward to the front of the first bag, shuffle laterally to the right until you pass the first bag, backpedal until you are behind the second bag, shuffle laterally to the right until you pass the second bag, then accelerate forward to the front of the third bag. Repeat this sequence for up to six bags.

3. As you pass the final bag, accelerate forward between the bags until you pass the first bag.

4. Rest for three minutes and repeat, starting from the opposite end.

5. Perform six repetitions.

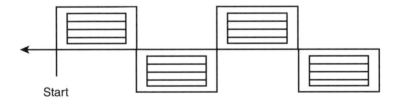

Start

LINEOUT EVASION

Purpose: To develop fast forward and backward movements for evading defenders during a lineout. This drill is appropriate for lineout jumpers and lifters.

Equipment and area: Twelve cones and a flat surface, preferably with grass.

Procedure: The goal is to move quickly by taking short, fast strides (usually two steps) from one cone to the next and then to perform a lineout-specific jump. Position yourself at 45 degrees to the opposition and line of touch, and jump using a double-foot takeoff. You can also practice a "dummy jump" by bending your knees and initiating the jumping arm movement to fake jumping and then moving forward or backward instead.

1. Position three sets of four cones one meter apart in a straight line, creating two lineout channels.

2. Drill 1. With your back to the lineout channel behind you and starting at A, backpedal to B, move forward to A, and jump. Rest for 10 seconds and repeat.

3. Drill 2. Facing toward A and starting at B, move forward to A, backpedal to B, move forward back to A, and jump. Rest for 10 seconds and repeat.

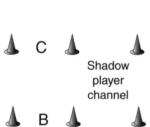

Shadow player channel

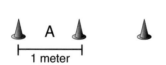

1 meter

4. Drill 3. Facing toward B and starting at C, backpedal to D, dummy jump, move forward to C, and jump. Rest for 10 seconds and repeat.

5. Drill 4. Facing toward B and starting at C, move forward to A, dummy jump and backpedal to B, and jump. Rest for 15 seconds and repeat.

6. Perform six sets of the four drills with one minute rest between drills and three minutes between sets.

Progression

- Include a lineout throw to increase the specificity of the drill.

- Lineout lifters will also benefit from this drill by following the jumper through the sequence and then supporting the jump. Lifters should focus on the hips of the jumper as they follow him or her up and down the channel.

- Have a second player simulate a lineout situation by shadowing the jumper during the drill to develop defensive lineout agility with a reactive agility drill. Do not inform the defender of the movements that the jumper will make.

SIDE STEP

Purpose: To develop an effective side step that minimizes loss of speed.

Equipment and area: Grassy area of a minimum of 10 by 30 meters, four cones, and a rugby ball.

Procedure: The objective is to convince the defender that you, the attacker, are going to run past on the outside, but then suddenly sidestep to change direction and accelerate on the inside.

1. As you run with the ball in your hands, accelerate toward the defender. When there is only five meters between you, drift toward the defender's right shoulder, taking small steps and looking in the direction you're traveling.

2. While maintaining your running speed, drop your right shoulder and plant your right foot down hard to the right. Push hard off your right foot and change direction to accelerate to the left, stepping to the inside and "wrong-footing" the defender (see figure a). Rest for one minute.

3. Repeat the drill, but step off your left foot. Rest for one minute.

4. Repeat the drill, but have the defender come from the right or left corner of the grid (see figure b). Make the same movements, first

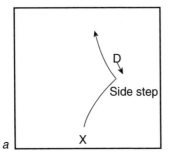

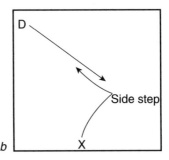

running toward the defender's outside before stepping back inside by dynamically planting the ball of your foot and accelerating away. Rest for one minute, then repeat with the defender coming from the other corner.

5. Perform each variation twice, for a total of eight repetitions.

Key points

- The later you make the side step, the less chance the defender will have to change direction and tackle you.
- Imagine you have a sore left toe, encouraging a "limp" on the left foot before stepping. This helps introduce an effective right foot plant.

Progression

- Try a more dramatic, advanced side step that requires greater support from the inside leg and a double-leg skip. Just before you make the side step, both of your feet are off the ground at the same time. As you land on, for example, your right (outside) foot, immediately plant your left (inside) foot toward the left so that it supports your right leg by pushing toward the left. The inside leg is therefore closer to the outside leg and, instead of preparing you to take a wide step, both feet propel you to the left.
- Step in any direction you choose, making it a reactive instead of a programmed sidestep drill.

Dan's Top Tip

The best side step is a hop and a step. You can fix a defense with a short hop to the right, a feinted step to the left (not too big a step, and keep your legs under your body weight), and an explosive movement to the left at a tangent, concentrating on accelerating away. Or hop left, then feint and accelerate to the right. Walk through the steps first to learn the movement, then try running. Also, play a game of Touch Rugby in which everyone who receives the ball must perform an effective side step.

IN-AND-OUT SWERVE

Purpose: To develop an effective in-and-out swerve that minimizes loss of speed.

Equipment and area: Grassy area of a minimum of 10 by 30 meters, four cones, and a rugby ball.

Procedure: It takes more time to swerve than to sidestep, but it is easier to swerve at high speed. In this drill, the attacker tries to convince the defender that he will take an inside running line, but then swerves to the outside. Whereas a side step is a sudden movement, a swerve is performed over several strides so the running speed can be maintained.

1. As you run with the ball in your hands, accelerate over 15 meters toward the defender. When you are 5 to 10 meters away from the defender, drift toward the defender's right shoulder and look in the direction you are traveling.

2. While maintaining your running speed, gradually change direction to your right. Then, place the ball in your outside (right) hand and push hard off your left foot to accelerate to your right without losing speed. Rest for two minutes.

3. Repeat the drill, but swerve to your left. Rest for two minutes.

4. Repeat the drill, but have the defender come from the right or left corner of the grid. Make the same movements, first running toward the defender's outside shoulder before swerving away by dynamically planting the ball of your foot and accelerating.

Progression: Instead of having the defender let the attacker pass, allow tackling.

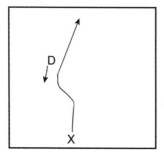

HIT AND SPIN!

Purpose: To develop the ability to spin 360 degrees to protect the ball and evade defenders.

Equipment and area: Grassy area of 5 by 20 meters, two pad holders, and four cones.

Procedure

1. Position two pad holders 5 meters apart. Place a start cone 5 meters in front of the first pad holder and a finish cone 5 meters beyond the second pad holder. Place another cone half a meter to the right of the first pad holder and the fourth one half a meter to the left of the second pad holder. The space between the pad holder and cone is the *target pivot area.*

2. Start by carrying the ball from the start cone with both hands and accelerating toward the first pad holder. As you come to the final few strides before the pad holder, swerve slightly to your right as you gradually reduce your stride length and body height and hold the ball tight against your body with your right arm.

3. Swerve into the target pivot area to the right of the pad holder and drop your left shoulder. Plant your left foot in the target pivot area at 45 degrees to the pad holder and make contact with the pad. At the same time, dynamically rotate your body 360 degrees clockwise by pushing off your planted (left) foot and, keeping your body low, pushing your back against the pad to help you make the turn. Hold the ball tightly against your body.

4. After completing the spin, accelerate toward the second pad holder and repeat the movement, but this time, swerve to the left of the pad holder and spin counterclockwise. Accelerate to the end cone to finish the drill.

5. Rest for two minutes, then repeat five more times.

RUNNING CLOCK DRILL

Purpose: To develop speed and agility with a multidirectional course that includes down-ups.

Equipment and area: Grassy area of a minimum of 10 by 30 meters, measuring tape, 14 poles, and a stopwatch.

Procedure: See page 25 in chapter 3 for instructions for the Running Clock Drill.

1. Complete one lap of the course as a speed and agility drill and record how long it takes you.

2. Rest until you have fully recovered and then repeat for five laps.

Progression: Wear a vest weighted with 10 percent of your body weight. Alternate between weighted and unweighted repetitions of the course, resting for four minutes between each repetition.

REACTIVE SPEED AND AGILITY DRILLS

During reactive drills, the player must react to a stimulus such as a ball, defender, attacker, or instructions from a coach.

PARTNER REACT AND CATCH

Purpose: To develop reaction speed, rotational speed, and hand-eye coordination. This drill works on the reactions required for successfully catching the ball during competition.

Equipment and area: Flat surface and a rugby or tennis ball.

Procedure

1. Divide players into pairs, giving each pair a ball.

2. Drill 1. Partners stand facing each other, three meters apart. Player 1 holds the ball and Player 2 closes his eyes. As Player 1 passes the ball to Player 2, he simultaneously calls out Player 2's name so that Player 2 opens his eyes just in time to catch the ball. Player 1 must time the pass and call to Player 2 so that Player 2 sees the ball for only a split second before having to catch it. Make 10 passes, then

change roles. Do three sets. Make the drill more difficult by lobbing the ball to the left or right of your partner, or high or low, before calling out your partner's name. This encourages reactive foot speed.

3. Drill 2. Repeat drill 1, but stand on one leg. Vary your pass slightly so that your partner can remain on one leg and reach for the pass.

4. Drill 3. Repeat drill 1, but Player 2 must keep his eyes closed until he catches the ball. Players should stand with hands cupped at the waist, ready to catch the ball as soon as it makes contact with the hands. Make 10 passes and then change roles. Do three sets. Make the drill more difficult by having Player 2 stand on one leg.

5. Drill 4. Player 1 stands holding a ball three meters behind Player 2. As Player 1 lobs the ball, he calls Player 2's name. Player 2 jumps and turns—feet must leave the floor—to catch the ball before it hits the ground. The first passes in the drill should be easy to catch, but Player 1 should gradually begin to release the ball earlier to increase the challenge. Make 10 passes and then change roles. Do three sets.

Progression

- Give your partner less time to open his eyes before catching the ball (drills 1, 2, and 4).

- Vary the passes, making some low, high, or wide (drills 1, 2, and 4).

- Use a smaller ball, such as a tennis or golf ball, to improve visual acuity. When the rugby ball is reintroduced, it will feel easier to catch.

Dan's Top Tip

For passing drills, use a tennis ball or golf ball to improve your hand-eye coordination and visual acuity. Start with a tennis ball, change to a golf ball, and then perform the drills with a rugby ball. The rugby ball will seem easier to catch because of its larger size.

ONE-ON-ONE TAG

Purpose: To improve offensive and defensive agility and reaction.

Equipment and area: Grassy area of a minimum of 10 by 20 meters, four cones, a tag belt or rugby ball, and a stopwatch.

Procedure: The goal of this drill for the defender is to grab the tag from the attacker's tag belt as soon as possible. The attacker tries to keep the tag for as long as possible.

1. Create a 10-meter square with four cones and position the players at opposite sides.

2. On the start command, the defender chases the tag holder as the latter moves quickly, making frequent changes in direction and turning to protect the tag belt from the defender. The tag holder cannot leave the square.

3. Record the time it takes for the defender to get the tag.

4. Rest for two to four minutes (depending on how long it took to get the tag), then change roles and repeat.

Progression

- Change from tagging to tackling.
- Increase the size of the square to 15 square meters.
- Use a rugby ball instead of a tag belt—attacker tries to protect the ball while the defender aims to touch the ball.

ONE-ON-ONE SHADOW TAG

Purpose: To improve offensive and defensive agility and reaction.

Equipment and area: Grassy area of a minimum of 10 square meters, six cones, and a tag belt.

Procedure

1. Create a 10-square-meter channel with two rows of three cones placed 5 meters apart. The rows are 10 meters apart.

2. The attacking player stands between the rows of cones at one side of the square and the defending player stands between the rows in the middle of the channel. The coach stands at the opposite side of the square.

3. Using arm signals, the coach directs the lateral movements of the attacking player as the defending player shadows the attacking player. For example, when the coach raises his or her left arm, the attacker moves to that side and the defender follows.

4. The coach randomly claps to signal to the attacking player to try to run past the defender without losing the tag.

5. Rest for two minutes. Then change roles and repeat for 10 drills in total.

Progression

- Change from tagging to tackling.
- Increase the size of the square to 15 square meters.

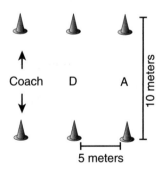

FETCH!

Purpose: To develop quick changes in direction while using ball skills. This partner drill is also part of a circuit in the Fuel Mix section.

Equipment and area: Grassy area of 20 square meters, four cones, and two balls.

Procedure

1. Create a 10-meter square with four cones.
2. The ball passer lobs or rolls a ball around the grid for the active player to pass back as quickly as possible.
3. As one ball is returning to the passer, the passer lobs or rolls a second ball. The passer should not have to move to catch the return pass.
4. Perform the drill for 15 to 20 seconds or for a specific number of passes. Rest for 2 minutes.
5. Change roles and perform 5 drills in total.

Key points

- This drill requires high levels of passing and catching skill.
- The active player should take small steps and maintain a low body position to facilitate quickly changing direction.

Progression

- Enlarge the grid to 20 square meters.
- Use two passers, each with a ball, instead of one passer with two balls. Passers may then move around the grid before releasing the ball.

CONTACT CHANNEL

Purpose: To improve the ability to maintain balance, foot speed, and control following contact.

Equipment and area: Grassy area of 10 by 20 meters, four pad holders, and 20 cones.

Procedure

1. Create a 20-meter-long, 2-meter-wide channel with the cones. Leave two one-meter spaces in each line of cones through which the pad holders can attack.

2. At the start command, carry a ball in both hands and run the course between the cones (the middle of the channel). As the pad holder pushes you and tries to disrupt your balance and footwork, try to resist and stay inside the channel.

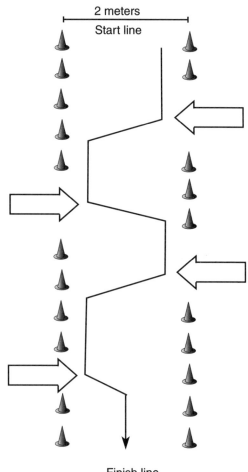

3. Perform the drill at half pace initially, then progress to full speed.

4. Rest for three minutes, then repeat for six runs.

Key points

- Pad holders should target the hip-to-shoulder area. The contact should start off light and gradually increase in force as your performance improves.

- The runner must run close to the side cones to allow the pad holders to stay outside the channel.

Progression

- Encourage the runner to "hit and spin" off the pad holder.

- Have pad holders increase the force of their pushing.

TEAM AGILITY COURSES

Purpose: To develop agility by using a competitive agility course. Two or more players can run a relay race. Courses can also be used for individual training. Allowing players maximum rest between repetitions of a course ensures that players run the course at or close to maximum pace. Repeating the courses with short recovery times is suitable for specific fuel mix conditioning.

Equipment and area: Grassy area, foot-speed ladders, cones, poles, tackle bags, tackle pads, mini hurdles (15 centimeters), tag belts, a rugby ball, and a stopwatch.

Procedure

1. Prepare your course using the detailed diagrams. The players start each course lying on the floor behind the start line.

2. On the start command, all players follow the course (or their portion of it if it is a relay race) to the finish line. If it is a relay, use a ball as the baton.

3. Record players' times as agility performance scores. Allow time for a full recovery between races. Repeat runs for fuel mix conditioning.

Course 1 (see figure a)

1. Start on the floor to the left of the mini hurdle or pad with a rugby ball on the floor just in front of you.

2. On the "go" command, stand up quickly, collect the ball, and perform four fast lateral hops back and forth over the mini hurdle or pad.

3. On landing from the fourth hop, sprint through the ladder with one foot in each square (alternative ladder drills may also be used).

4. Sprint out of the ladder and around all the poles until you reach the pad holder. Perform a hit and spin on the tackle pad held by a player or coach, sprint through the end cones, and pop the ball to the next player waiting between the cones. Player 2 repeats the course but in the opposite direction, starting with a hit and spin (pivoting off the right foot and running to the left of the first pole) and finishing with four lateral hops over the hurdle before placing the ball on the ground in front of the next player.

5. Repeat the relay until every player has performed one lap of the course in each direction. Compete against other teams who run a mirrored version of the course.

Course 1

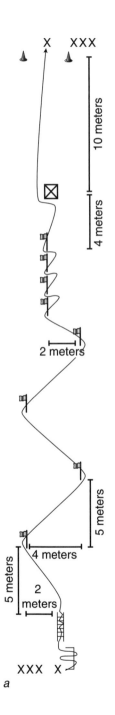

Tackle pad

Ladder

Mini hurdle
or pad

a

179

Course 2 (see figure b)

Use two teams of equal number (at least three per team). Team 1 acts as attackers (run the course) and wear tag belts; team 2 acts as defenders. Each team member needs a ball, which is collected following the tackle.

Course 2

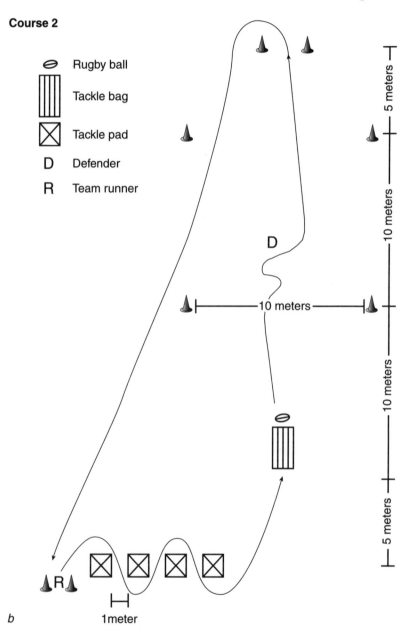

b

A player from team 2 acts as a defender in the 10-by-10-meter grid of the course. The defender aims to remove the tag belt of the runner (or two-handed touch at waist height if tags are not available).

1. Player 1 starts by running between the pads while facing forward at all times (move forward, laterally, and backward between pads).
2. Following the final pad, player 1 tackles the bag and immediately gets up to collect the ball, which was resting on top of the bag and is dislodged by the tackle. With the ball, the player races to the two end cones, evading the defender on route—specifically, avoids losing the tag belt or being touched.
3. Once the player is between the end cones he or she places the ball on the ground, as if scoring a try, and races back to the finish line, which is adjacent to the start line. The next team member starts the course as soon as player 1 crosses the finish line.
4. Perform the relay until every team member has run the course. Repeat the course with team 2 as attackers and team 1 as defenders.
5. The winning team is the team that completes the course in the shortest time. However, five seconds are added to a team's course time for each player who has a tag removed or touched.

Key points

- The defending team is responsible for replacing the tackle bag and another ball to the original position following each tackle.
- Start a stopwatch as the team begins the race and record the time as the last team member crosses the finish line. You may also record individual course times.
- Defending teams must change defenders in the grid for each attacking player during the course.

SAMPLE SPEED AND AGILITY TRAINING PROGRAM

The following sample program is designed to improve speed and agility and includes programmed and reactive drills. Ensure that you have at least one day between sessions and that you are fresh when starting these sessions.

Six-Week Speed and Agility Program

Guidelines

- Perform two to three sessions per week, alternating between sessions 1 and 2.
- Begin your warm-up with control and skipping (jump rope) drills.
- Lineout forwards should replace Hollow Sprints with the Lineout Evasion Drill, performing two repetitions of each drill with one minute rest between drills. Repeat for two sets with two minutes' rest between sets.

SESSION 1

Drill	Sets	Repetitions or distance	Rest between sets
Forward Skipping	3	1 × 20 m	30 s.
Lateral Skipping (left and right)	3	2 × 10 m	30 s.
Body Lean Accelerations	3	4	30 s.
Top-Five Ladder Drills	2	1 × each drill with walk-back recovery	2 min.
Medicine Ball Chuck and Chase	5	1	3 min.
Hollow Sprints	3	1	4 min.
Running Clock Drill	3	1	4 min.
One-on-One Tag	3	1	90 s.

SESSION 2

Drill	Sets	Repetitions or distance	Rest between sets
Reach for Balance!	3	4 reps of drill 1 and 2	90 s.
Backward Running	3	1 × 10 m	45 s.
Bag Drill	3	1	3 min.
Side Step	3	2 (left and right steps)	3 min.
In-and-Out Swerve	3	2 (left and right steps)	3 min.
Fetch!	6	1 (10 s.)	2 min.

CHAPTER 8

FUEL MIX DRILLS

The aim of fuel mix drills is to

improve players' capacity to generate energy and resist fatigue so they can perform effectively for the duration of the game. Rugby is a high-intensity sport in which players undertake multiple sprints and various strength and power movements that require the rapid production of energy. This energy is produced by the anaerobic and aerobic systems, either exclusively or at the same time—hence the term *fuel mix*.

Just how much anaerobic and aerobic fuel an individual needs during a game depends on several factors, including how long the ball is in play, the distance and speed at which the player runs, the player's overall conditioning level, and the level of competition. The importance of these factors varies among playing positions, with each position placing unique demands on the player. Forwards, for example, require high levels of anaerobic fuel for rucking, scrummaging, and driving play. Because their rest periods are relatively short, however, their systems must contribute more aerobic fuel to compensate at times when the anaerobic system has not been able to recover sufficiently.

ENDURANCE AND STAMINA TRAINING

Traditionally, fuel mix conditioning has been called *endurance* or *stamina training*. Although these terms are applicable, they suggest—erroneously—that rugby is an aerobic sport and that training should include a high volume of aerobic drills, like steady-state distance runs. We prefer to use the terms *fuel mix* and *repeatability* to emphasize that the anaerobic energy system must make a major contribution while the ball is in play.

To conform to the principle of specificity, fuel mix training drills must reflect the start–stop nature of rugby by taking into account the ratio of work-to-rest times. In addition, they must integrate movement strength and power activities to match the fuel mix demands of rugby.

ANAEROBIC ENERGY

Anaerobic energy production relies on two subsystems, one producing alactic energy and the other, lactic energy. Alactic energy—the most powerful of the two—is the fuel of choice for explosive movements such as tackling and sprinting. However, alactic energy is produced only for short periods (about 5 to 15 seconds), after which the lactic system takes over. The lactic system produces speed- and power-generating energy, but it also produces a waste product known as lactic acid that causes fatigue.

The duration of recovery between periods of play in a game dictates how quickly these anaerobic fuels are replenished. If recovery is too short, more lactic acid is produced and increasing support is needed from the aerobic energy system, which results in reduced power output.

Training drills designed to help players increase the power and capacity of their anaerobic systems include high-effort interval running and circuit training. By raising the capacity of the alactic system, the threshold at which lactic acid is produced can be raised. Training the lactic acid system causes adaptations that allow muscles to remove lactic acid more quickly and to tolerate higher acid levels. These drills also improve fuel mix fitness, because the aerobic system also contributes and develops as players perform them.

AEROBIC ENERGY

The aerobic system fuels activities that require a submaximal rate of energy production, such as walking and jogging. Because most actions in rugby demand a rapid supply of energy, the aerobic pathway is simply too slow and cannot provide enough power for rucking, sprinting, and tackling. However, a sound level of aerobic fitness is necessary for players to maintain a high work rate during competition, because the aerobic system's major role is to help the anaerobic systems to recover. Players' heavy breathing during recovery periods to increase their oxygen uptake illustrates the anaerobic system's reliance on the aerobic system for recovery.

Walking and jogging account for at least 60 percent of the activity in a rugby match, and aerobic fuel alone sustains these movements. In combination with anaerobic fuel, it also sustains high-speed running in well-conditioned players.

Developing aerobic conditioning with long-distance running is not specific, and may even have a negative impact on strength and speed. General fuel mix drills, including interval running and circuit training drills, more effectively enhance the aerobic system's performance by challenging the production of aerobic fuel. In these drills, the aerobic system is the dominant energy provider, but the anaerobic energy system also contributes.

Fuel mix conditioning combines drills that challenge the aerobic and anaerobic energy systems, and often both at the same time. The fuel mix fitness tests in chapter 3 should be used to assess players' levels of aerobic fitness (Three-Kilometer Run) and anaerobic fitness (Running Clock Drill). Those findings will determine which type of fuel mix training system should be emphasized in the training program.

FUEL MIX TRAINING SYSTEMS

A fuel mix training system is either *general* or *specific*. General fuel mix drills involve work intervals that are longer than those experienced in competition and energy is provided by the lactic and aerobic systems. Players' running speed and movement intensity should be at 60 to 80 percent of maximum.

General fuel mix drills also include strength endurance circuits to improve movement pattern strength and stability endurance. Overloading the muscles responsible for these movements improves their ability to repeat the movements, which also helps to reduce the chances of injury. Cross-training methods such as cycling and swimming are also classified as general fuel mix drills, but they should be used sparingly because their movement patterns are not rugby-related.

Specific fuel mix drills use high- and maximal-intensity exercise and the movement patterns and work-to-rest ratio of competition. They emphasize fast running speeds and rugby-specific movements such as driving, tackling, and jumping. The alactic and lactic anaerobic systems are the main suppliers of energy during these drills, with the aerobic system aiding in recovery between drills.

RECONDITIONING FUEL MIX FITNESS

As they undergo rehabilitation for an injury, players must try to minimize loss in their fuel mix fitness level. Drills that do not involve the injured body part should begin as soon as possible. For example, players with shoulder injuries can perform lower-body endurance drills and those with leg injuries can keep up with upper-body endurance drills.

Lower-body endurance drills:

- Cycling or stepping
- Swimming without using your arms
- Fast walking
- High-repetition leg-based resistance and pattern strength drills

Upper-body endurance drills:

- Swimming without using your legs
- High-repetition upper-body resistance drills
- Arm crank devices
- Speedball and punch-bag circuits

Depending on how long rehabilitation takes, players should progress from general to specific fuel mix drills before returning to full rugby training and competition. A fuel mix fitness test (see chapter 3) will measure reversibility in conditioning and can be used to assess whether a player is fit enough to return to competition.

Fuel Mix Training Guidelines

The type, frequency, and volume of fuel mix training drills included in a training plan depend largely on the individual's level of fuel mix conditioning. The greater the level of fuel mix fitness, the higher should be the intensity and volume of these drills in a fuel mix training session. Table 8.1 identifies three categories of conditioning status based on training age (the length of time that a player has actively been training) and performance during a fuel mix fitness test. A player's conditioning status dictates the number of repetitions and the length and number of rest periods when performing fuel mix drills.

Table 8.1   Fuel Mix Conditioning Categories

Conditioning status	Training age/Fitness test rating
Basic	Untrained or training age of 0 to 6 months/Poor rating on Running Clock Drill and poor or fair rating on the Three-Kilometer Run
Intermediate	Training age of 6 months to 1 year/Good rating on the Three-Kilometer Run and fair or good rating on the Running Clock Drill
Advanced	Training age of more than 1 year/Good to excellent rating on the Running Clock Drill

Interval Training

During interval training, players perform bouts of running for a specified period of time or distance. They are allowed to rest between intervals to facilitate and manipulate recovery; the longer the rest interval, the greater the level of recovery.

The length of a standard rugby pitch (100 meters) is used to describe interval distances. For example, if the interval distance is four, the player runs four lengths of a rugby pitch starting and finishing on the try lines (or 400 meters). On shorter-than-average pitches, the dead ball line to dead ball line is more appropriate. A running track can also be used by multiplying the number of pitch lengths by 100 meters.

Maximum Training Speed

Several methods of indicating exercise intensity can be used during fuel mix training, including heart rate, rate of perceived exertion, and the maximum training speed principle. This chapter uses the latter method. *Maximum training speed* is defined as the running or exercise intensity that will produce the best performance over an entire set. For example, if a player performing six repetitions of a running interval with 30 seconds' rest between them makes an all-out or maximum effort in the first two intervals, his or her performance in the subsequent intervals will suffer markedly. Maximum training speed, therefore, is the amount of effort a player expends when "pacing" himself or herself so that subsequent intervals can be completed at a similar speed and effort level.

Dan's Top Tip

One frequently overlooked aspect of fuel mix training is running technique. Running with correct posture and style has a significant effect on movement efficiency. By simply improving your running technique, you will improve your fuel mix conditioning. See chapter 7 for guidelines on basic running technique.

Warm-Up and Active Rest

Warm up thoroughly before performing fuel mix drills. Use active rest techniques during allocated rest periods to encourage blood to flow back to the heart instead of pooling. Avoid sitting or standing still between drills.

GENERAL FUEL MIX CONDITIONING DRILLS

General fuel mix conditioning develops the aerobic and lactic anaerobic energy systems.

THREE-MINUTE INTERVALS

Purpose: To develop the aerobic and lactic systems. In this drill, players run at threshold running speed, which is the line between aerobic and anaerobic energy supply.

Equipment and area: Off-road path, rugby pitch, or track; a stopwatch.

Procedure

1. Run continuously for three minutes, then walk for two minutes for recovery. Perform the specified number of repetitions and sets according to your conditioning status (see table 8.2).

2. Determine your average three-minute distance by adding together the interval distances and dividing by the number of intervals. Use this distance as a minimum target for your next Three-Minute Intervals session.

Key point: Apply the maximum training speed principle so that all the interval distances are similar.

Progression: After your fourth Three-Minute Intervals training session, reduce the interval to two minutes and the rest between repetitions to one and a half minutes. Increase your running speed to make up for the reduction in running time.

Table 8.2   Three-Minute Intervals

Conditioning status	Interval (min.:s.)	Repetitions	Rest between repetitions (min.:s.)	Sets	Rest between sets (min.:s.)
Basic	3:00	4	2:00	1	—
Intermediate	3:00	3	2:00	2	3:00
Advanced	3:00	4	2:00	2	4:00

FIGURE-EIGHT INTERVALS

Purpose: To develop aerobic capacity and lactic acid tolerance. This drill introduces changes in direction.

Equipment and area: Rugby pitch and a stopwatch.

Procedure

1. Follow the course, as illustrated in the figure, until you complete a figure-eight circuit of the pitch. Perform the specified number of repetitions and sets according to your conditioning status (see table 8.3).

2. Determine your average figure-eight interval time by adding together the interval times and dividing by the number of intervals. Use this time as a maximum time to beat for your next Figure-Eight Intervals session.

Key point: Apply the maximum training speed principle so that all the interval times are similar.

Progression: Add an interval to each subsequent session.

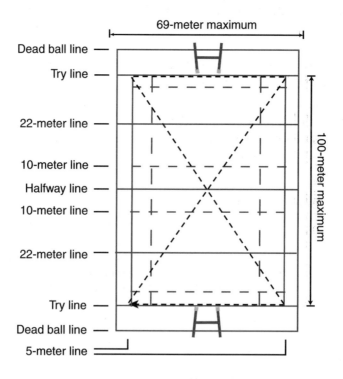

Table 8.3 Figure-Eight Intervals

Conditioning status	Repetitions	Rest between repetitions (min.:s.)	Sets	Rest between sets (min.:s.)
Basic	6	1:00	1	—
Intermediate	4	0:45	2	2:00
Advanced	6	0:45	2	2:00

PYRAMID INTERVALS

Purpose: To stimulate production of varying levels of aerobic and anaerobic energy by using fluctuating interval distances. This session replicates the various work and rest periods typically experienced during competitive rugby.

Equipment and area: Rugby pitch or a track and a stopwatch.

Procedure

1. In a Pyramid Intervals session, players run lengths of a pitch (100 meters). The first interval involves running four continuous lengths of the pitch, followed by 40 seconds' rest. For the second interval, three lengths are run, followed by 40 seconds' rest, and so on, as set out in table 8.4, until you finish the set by running the seventh interval, which is four lengths.

Table 8.4 Pyramid Intervals

Conditioning status	Interval distances	Rest between intervals (min.:s.)	Sets	Rest between sets (min.:s.)
Basic	4-3-2-1-2-3-4	0:40	1	—
Intermediate	4-3-2-1-2-3-4	0:40	1.5	2:00
Advanced	4-3-2-1-2-3-4	0:40	2	2:00

2. Rest for the period indicated for your conditioning status and repeat for the specified number of sets. Players at the intermediate level of conditioning should stop after the fourth interval (one length) of their second set.

3. Compare your times for the first and last intervals (both are four pitch lengths) of each set. Try to reduce the difference between these times.

Progression: Increase your running intensity by increasing the period of rest between intervals to 1 minute.

CIRCUIT TRAINING

Circuit training integrates repeated core stabilization and pattern strength drills with interval running. This is an important progression from purely running-based fuel mix training because it more fully replicates the fuel mix demands of rugby.

It is very important that circuit training not be introduced until a phase of core stabilization and pattern strength training has been completed. Guidelines for these exercises are in chapter 6.

Circuit drills combine movements selected from the core stabilization and strength drills in chapter 6 (see table 8.5). Introducing drills such as the Rotating Ramp and Push-Up and Pull to fuel mix circuits is also an ideal core stabilization progression. The circuit challenges core muscle control and endurance as players breathe heavily, replicating the core stability demands of competitive rugby.

Table 8.5   Circuit Drills

Movement	Guidelines
1. Push-up	Perform a standard body weight push-up.
2. Multidirectional Lunge	See page 97 for drill description. One lunge in each of the four directions equals one repetition.
3. Rotating Ramp	See page 86 for drill description. Hold each of the four positions for 5 s. for one repetition.
4. Lunge and Dummy Pass	See page 96 for drill description.
5. Push-Up and Pull	See page 95 for drill description.
6. Reach and Touch Down	Alternate legs. See page 100 for drill description.
7. Shoulder Step-Up	See page 94 for drill description. Use a tackle bag or partner as the step.
8. Arm and Leg Raise	See page 85 for drill description.
9. Down-Up	Bend your knees to perform a controlled fall to the floor and land on your side. Immediately stand up, using both arms and legs. Alternate sides.

PITCH LINE CIRCUIT

Purpose: To increase players' ability to repeat stability, strength, and running drills. This drill is a step closer to more specific fuel mix drills.

Equipment and area: Rugby pitch, tackle bag, and a stopwatch.

Procedure

1. At each line on a rugby pitch, as shown in the figure, perform the correspondingly numbered movement from table 8.5. Do the number of repetitions stipulated for your conditioning status (see table 8.6), then move on to the next movement at the prescribed running speed. The circuit is complete when you have performed exercise 9.

2. After completing a circuit, return to the start line at the prescribed running speed, then rest and repeat for three sets.

Table 8.6   Pitch Line Circuit

Conditioning status	Repetitions	Sets	Rest between sets (min.:s.)	Running speed between lines
Basic	4	3	2:00	Fast walk
Intermediate	6	3	1:30	Jog
Advanced	8	3	1:00	Three-quarters-pace run

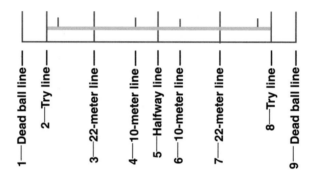

Progression: Add a repetition to each exercise at each subsequent session.

SPECIFIC FUEL MIX DRILLS

Specific fuel mix training drills stimulate and overload the anaerobic energy system by including demands and movement patterns typical of competitive rugby. Drills are performed at or at close to maximum speed and intensity. In contrast to general fuel mix drills, the aerobic system supports the anaerobic systems during specific fuel mix drills.

RUGBY INTERVAL DRILLS

These drills involve multidirectional running and work-to-rest ratios similar to those experienced during rugby. They are high-intensity drills, and the aim is to run at speeds greater than three-quarters pace.

RUNNING CLOCK DRILL

Purpose: To develop rugby-specific fuel mix conditioning. A variation of this drill is also used as a fuel mix conditioning test. Details and standards are in chapter 3, Rugby Fitness Testing.

On this multidirectional course, players perform repetitions separated by rest periods of lengths dictated by the amount of time taken to perform a repetition and the time registered on a running clock. The total time needed to complete all of the repetitions provides feedback on fuel mix performance.

The four combinations of course repetitions set out in tables 8.7 through 8.10 can be used to make the drill position-specific. Options 1 and 2 are suitable for forwards because they involve longer work intervals and shorter recovery periods. Option 3 is appropriate for inside backs, whereas option 4 is appropriate for outside backs because they involve work and rest in ratios similar to those the players will experience during competition. Players performing any of the four options should rest for four minutes after completing a set and then repeat it. Apply the maximum training speed principle.

Equipment and area: Grassy area of a minimum of 10 by 30 meters, measuring tape, 14 poles, two stopwatches, and two coaches.

Procedure

1. Perform one lap of the course as part of your warm-up to familiarize yourself with the route (see steps 2 through 6 for course details). See page 27 for a diagram of the course.

Table 8.7 Option 1: Pyramid Running Clock Drill

Running clock time (min.:s.)	Number of laps
0:00	1
1:00	2
2:30	3
4:45	2
6:30	1

Table 8.8 Option 2: Maximum Ball-in-Play Time

Running clock time (min.:s.)	Number of laps
0:00	3
2:00	3
4:15	3
6:30	3
9:00	3

Table 8.9 Option 3: Fluctuating Ball-in-Play Time

Running clock time (min.:s.)	Number of laps
0:00	1
1:00	2
2:30	1
4:00	2
5:30	1

Table 8.10   Option 4: Running Fast Scores Tries!

Running clock time (min.:s.)	Number of laps
0:00	1
1:30	1
3:00	2
5:30	1
7:00	1

2. Stand at the start line between poles P1 and P2, facing forward (that is, looking down the length of the course).

3. On the start command, shuffle (run laterally) left to P4, backpedal from P4 to P5, shuffle right to P6, and perform a down-up behind and between P6 and P7.

4. Sprint straight and then around P8, P9, and P10 and through P11 and P12 to P13 and P14. Turn around and perform a down-up behind and between P13 and P14.

5. Sprint between P11 and P12, then back between P13 and P14 and do another down-up.

6. Sprint to the finish line between P1 and P3.

7. This equals one lap of the course. When multiple laps are to be performed, immediately run around P1 after crossing the finish line and repeat the course shuffling from the start line to P4.

8. The running clock's time dictates when you start each set and the rest time between sets.

9. Keep track of your time for each lap or group of laps and monitor them for performance feedback.

AGILITY COURSES FOR SPECIFIC FUEL MIX DRILLS

The two team agility courses that appear on pages 178 through 181 in chapter 7 can also be used for running clock circuits. Simply substitute those courses' movements for the ones in the Running Clock Drill and complete them according to the instructions just given for the four options for players in various positions.

SPEED ENDURANCE INTERVALS

Speed endurance intervals are intense running sessions fueled almost exclusively by anaerobic energy (alactic and lactic). These drills involve periods of exertion and running speeds similar to those in competitive rugby, but far longer rest periods between intervals to permit full or almost-full recovery. The aim is to run each interval as quickly as possible—do *not* apply the maximum training speed principle.

Performing these drills subjects muscles to levels of lactic acid that are equal to or higher than the levels produced during competitive rugby, overloading the anaerobic systems. Do not perform these sessions more than twice per week.

These drills are suitable only for players who have several months of fuel mix conditioning under their belt.

HILL INTERVALS

Purpose: To improve anaerobic energy capacity with high-intensity running against resistance (on a gradient).

Equipment and area: 60- to 70-meter-long slope with a gradient of 7.5 to 10 degrees and a stopwatch.

Procedure

1. Starting at the bottom of the slope, accelerate up it, focusing on powerfully driving your arms and legs.

2. Walk back down the slope, then once you reach the start line, rest for the amount of time specified in table 8.11, according to your conditioning level.

Table 8.11   Hill Intervals

Conditioning status	Repetitions	Rest between repetitions (min.:s.)	Sets	Rest between sets (min.:s.)
Intermediate	4	3:00	2	4:00
Advanced	6	2:30	2	4:00

3. Keep track of your times and try to minimize the difference between your first and last repetitions. This is a reflection of speed endurance.

Progression: Add a repetition to every third training session to reach a maximum of 7 for intermediate players and 10 for advanced players.

TRACK 233S—DAN'S FAVORITE DRILL

Purpose: To improve anaerobic energy capacity with high-intensity running.

Equipment and area: Running track or area 233 meters long and a stopwatch.

Procedure

1. A track is the most suitable venue for this drill. Start 33 meters beyond the 200-meter start line. Run each interval at maximum speed and maintain correct running technique.

2. Rest for the indicated length of time (see table 8.12), then repeat for the specified number of repetitions.

3. Keep track of your times and try to minimize the difference between your first and last repetitions. This is a reflection of your level of fatigue.

Table 8.12   Track 233s

Conditioning status	Repetitions	Rest between repetitions (min.:s.)
Intermediate	3	4:00
Advanced	4	5:00

Dan's Top Tip

The masochist in me loves 233-meter speed endurance drills. The lactic acid that builds up in your running muscles and the oxygen debt that is incurred remind me that I will never get that tired in a game. And that's exactly the idea: to build up tolerance to lactic acid so your body can repeatedly perform at high speeds without losing its edge.

SPEED ENDURANCE INTERVAL COMBINATIONS

Table 8.13 lists alternative interval combinations for running over flat ground. The shorter the interval distance, the greater should be your running speed and, consequently, the percentage of energy supplied by the alactic system. Keep track of your times and try to minimize the difference between your first and last repetitions of each set.

Table 8.13   Speed Endurance Interval Combinations

Conditioning status	Interval (m)	Repetitions	Rest between repetitions (min.:s.)	Sets	Rest between sets (min.:s.)
Intermediate	150	4	2:00	2	3:00
Advanced	150	6	2:00	2	3:00
Intermediate	100	3	2:00	3	4:00
Advanced	100	3	2:00	4	4:00
Intermediate	60	3	1:00	4	4:00
Advanced	60	4	1:00	4	4:00
Intermediate	30	5	0:30	3	4:00
Advanced	30	7	0:30	3	4:00

INTEGRATED CIRCUIT DRILLS

Integrated circuit drills overload movement patterns experienced in competitive rugby. These movements—performed at a high intensity—include driving, mauling, tackling, and jumping.

Table 8.14 lists 13 movement pattern drills selected to form this integrated circuit.

Table 8.14   Integrated Circuit Drills

Movement	Guidelines
1. Maul ball 	Crouching, protect a rugby ball for 15 s. as your partner attempts to maul it away. Change roles and repeat. This equals 1 repetition.
2. Forward drive 	Have your partner hold a contact pad in front of you. Attack and drive your partner back 5 m. He or she should offer high resistance, but allow you to reach the 5 m cone within 5 s. Both of you immediately backpedal to the start line and repeat for 4 drives. Rest for 10 seconds, change roles, and repeat. This equals 1 repetition.
3. Turn it over 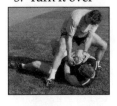	Lie on the ground protecting a rugby ball for 15 s. as your partner straddles you, attempting to maul the ball away. Change roles and repeat. This equals 1 repetition.
4. Fetch! 	As you stand inside a 10 m square, your partner rolls or lobs a rugby ball anywhere within the grid. Retrieve and return the ball as quickly as possible. Dive on the ball to get the ball when your partner rolls it on the floor. Perform the drill for 10 passes, then change roles and repeat. This equals 1 repetition.

(continued)

Table 8.14 *(continued)*

Movement	Guidelines
5. Hit 1-2-3 	Crouch in front of your partner as he or she holds a contact pad. Hit the pad and drive for 3 s. (which your partner counts out loud) before hitting the ground and correctly placing the ball away from or close to your body. Get up from the ground, grab the ball, and immediately repeat the drill for 6 hits, alternating the lead shoulder. Change roles and repeat. This equals 1 repetition.
6. Run and jump 	Lob a rugby ball for your partner to jump and catch, changing the direction frequently to change the catcher's running line. Perform the drill for 6 catches, change roles and repeat. This equals 1 repetition.
7. Sideways drive 	Follow the guidelines for the forward drive, but attack and hit the pad sideways, alternating left and right shoulders. Return to the start line by moving laterally.
8. Get up! Stay down! 	Lie facedown on the floor with your partner standing over you. Try to get up from the floor as your partner tries to prevent that by any means short of lying down on you—your partner must stay on his or her feet! Perform the drill for 15 s., change roles, and repeat. A player who succeeds in getting up within 15 s. repeats the drill until the 15 s. has expired. This equals 1 repetition.
9. Tackle shuttle 	Lie facedown 3 m from a tackle bag or partner holding a pad. Get up, stay low, and tackle the bag or pad holder, alternating the leading shoulder and focusing on driving the bag or pad holder back a few meters. Backpedal to the start line after each tackle. Perform the drill for 4 tackles, change roles, and repeat. This equals 1 repetition.

Table 8.14   *(continued)*

Movement	Guidelines
10. Multidirectional grid	Mark out a 10 m square. Starting at the bottom left corner, accelerate forward to the top left corner, shuffle laterally to the top right corner, backpedal to the bottom right corner, shuffle laterally back to the start corner, and sprint across the square to the top right corner. This equals 1 repetition.
11. Partner wrestle to the floor 	In a 3 m square, try to wrestle your partner to the floor as he or she protects a rugby ball and tries to stay standing. Perform the drill for 15 s., then change roles and repeat. This is not a tackling drill: Contact must be above waist height. Rest for 10 s., change roles, and repeat. This equals 1 repetition.
12. Backward drive 	Follow the guidelines for the forward drive, but attack and hit the pad with your back. After driving the pad holder 5 m, sprint forward back to the starting line. The pad holder must be careful not to suddenly stop resisting the push at the 5 m marker.
13. Hands-high drive 	Follow the guidelines for the forward drive, but attack and drive your partner at arm's length.

LUCKY 13 CIRCUIT

Purpose: To improve fuel mix conditioning for dynamic rugby movement patterns. This circuit integrates the 13 drills in table 8.14.

Equipment and area: Set up an area suitable for performing each Lucky 13 drill. Need a grassy area, tackle bag, contact pad, rugby ball, and a stopwatch.

Procedure

1. Organize players into pairs. Perform one repetition of each drill in table 8.14, resting for 30 seconds between drills. Completing the 13 drills equals one set.

2. Rest for the time indicated, then repeat for the number of sets specified for your conditioning status (see table 8.15).

Progression: Do two repetitions of each drill, still resting for 30 seconds between drills.

Table 8.15 Lucky 13 Circuit

Conditioning status	Rest between drills (min.:s.)	Sets	Rest between sets (min.:s.)
Basic	0:30	1	
Intermediate	0:30	2	3:00
Advanced	0:30	3	2:00

LUCKY 13 TRIANGLE CIRCUIT

Purpose: To improve specific fuel mix conditioning by integrating dynamic rugby movement pattern drills with partner racing intervals. This is similar to the Lucky 13 Circuit, but triangular running and walking intervals separate the drills.

Equipment and area: Rugby pitch, 10 cones, three poles, tackle bag, contact pad, rugby ball, and a stopwatch.

Procedure

1. Perform one repetition of drill 1 with your partner at cone A. As quickly as possible after finishing and with one of you leading the

other, race to cone B (at the midpoint of the 22-meter line) and back to cone E (in the opposite corner) at maximum training speed. Jog from cone E to F (the goalposts), turn around, and walk back to cone E.

2. Recover at cone E for the specified rest period before performing one repetition of drill 2, then race, with the other partner leading, from cone E to C (at the midpoint of the 10-meter line) and back to A. Once again, jog to the goalposts, turn around, and walk back to A before starting the rest period.

3. Proceed with the rest of the drills in the same manner, running a triangle race after each drill from alternating pitch corners (A and E) and changing the race distance each time. One complete circuit is summarized in table 8.17.

4. Intermediate and advanced players rest for five minutes and then continue for two and three sets, respectively (see table 8.16).

5. Keep track of your times for the triangle intervals for feedback on your performance.

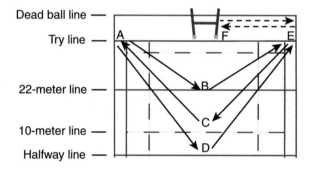

Table 8.16   Lucky 13 Triangle Circuit

Conditioning status	Rest after triangle intervals (min.:s.)	Sets	Rest between sets (min.:s.)
Basic	0:40	1	
Intermediate	0:30	2	5:00
Advanced	0:15	3	5:00

Table 8.17   Lucky 13 Triangle Circuit Sequence

Drill	Triangle race route
1	Cone A to B to E
2	Cone E to C to A
3	Cone A to D to E
4	Cone E to B to A
5	Cone A to C to E
6	Cone E to D to A
7	Cone A to B to E
8	Cone E to C to A
9	Cone A to D to E
10	Cone E to B to A
11	Cone A to C to E
12	Cone E to D to A
13	Cone A to B to E

TEAM CONDITIONING GAMES

Team games are excellent fuel mix conditioning drills that work on multidirectional running, passing, catching, attacking, and defensive skills. Teamwork and communication also improve with these drills, and players tend to enjoy the sessions, almost forgetting that there is a strong conditioning benefit.

Factors such as the pitch size, the number of players per team, and the duration of the game affect the energy system contributions and demands of the games. For example, Touch Rugby played by six-person teams across half a rugby pitch for 40 minutes is fueled by the lactic and aerobic energy systems. The same game played in 5-minute segments with 2 minutes of rest between segments will get players running at higher speeds. Use both continuous and segmental games in your conditioning program.

The following games are played with a rugby ball, but games like basketball, soccer, and netball can also be used as fuel mix drills.

GRID TAG

Purpose: This game integrates multidirectional running with passing, catching, attacking, and defending skills.

Number of players: Four to 20; start with 1 defender for every 3 attackers.

Equipment and area: Rugby ball, four cones, and an area of at least 15 square meters (larger for more players).

Procedure

1. Divide players into equal groups of attackers (A) and defenders (D). Start the game with a ratio of one defender to three attackers. D players not defending must stand outside the grid but may enter as defenders if tagged by a team member leaving the grid. The A players take the ball and, running anywhere within the grid, pass it in any direction as they try to avoid the D players.

2. D players score one point by tagging the attacker carrying the ball, either by touching him or her or taking the tag from the tag belt when players are in possession. D players also score one point if the attackers drop the ball or leave the grid.

3. After five minutes, A and D players switch roles and repeat the game.

4. Compare scores at the end to determine the winning team.

Progression

- Lower the ratio of attackers to defenders.
- Use a tennis ball instead of a rugby ball.
- Have D players tackle, rather than tag, the ball carrier.
- Introduce a rule that A players may not pass to an A player who has just passed the ball.

TOUCH RUGBY

Purpose: Touch Rugby—competitive rugby without the contact—integrates multidirectional running with passing, catching, attacking, and defending skills.

Number of players: Twelve.

Equipment and area: Rugby ball, half a rugby pitch, referee with a whistle, and a Sin Bin (penalty box).

Procedure

1. Divide players into two teams. Only six players from each team are allowed on the pitch at once, but reserve players can be substituted at any time from one side of the field. The active player must make contact with the reserve player behind the sideline to signify a substitution.

2. The game is played across the width of half a rugby pitch; the touch lines serve as the try lines.

3. Play starts and restarts at the center with a tap, which is performed by an attacking player who taps the ball on the ground with his or her foot and then picks it up. Similarly, when a team incurs a penalty, the attacking team taps the ball to return it to play. The defending team must retreat by at least five meters when the other team taps.

4. A try, which is worth one point, is scored by grounding the ball on or behind the try line.

5. To be legal, a touch can fall on any part of the body, clothing, or ball. Both hands must make contact, and the player must claim the touch by raising his or her hand and shouting, "Touch!" The referee is the sole judge of the legality of a touch and may overrule a claim.

6. When touched, the ball carrier must place the ball on the ground where the touch occurred. All defending players must retreat more than five meters in line with the mark of touch. The defending team cannot move forward until play restarts, nor interfere with play while retreating. The ball carrier then restarts play by performing a Play the Ball, in which he or she steps over the ball and controls the ball with one hand or foot to roll it back to a teammate. The ball cannot roll more than a meter.

7. The player who then picks up the ball (known as the dummy-half) can run, but if he or she is touched, a changeover occurs. The dummy-half cannot score; if this happens, a changeover (and Play the Ball) is awarded to the opposition.

8. After six touches, possession changes and play restarts with a tap. The attacking team now becomes the defending team and must retreat more than five meters beyond where the touch occurred, and they cannot move forward or interfere with play until play restarts. A restart occurs at the moment the ball is tapped or the dummy-half touches the ball at the Play the Ball. If there is no dummy-half in position (within one meter of the mark), defenders may advance from an onside position.

9. If the attacking player making a quick start is touched by an offside defender, play continues. If an attacking side gains no advantage, a penalty tap for the first down is given.

10. If a Play the Ball is taken within five meters of the score line, the defending players must retreat to have both of their feet behind the score line before they can make the touch. If the ball carrier is touched in the touchdown zone before grounding the ball, the touch counts and play is restarted on the five-meter line. Defenders cannot delay the game by deliberately delaying a Play the Ball.

11. If the ball is dropped or if the ball carrier crosses the sideline before being touched, a change of possession takes place with a Play the Ball.

12. If the defending team tries unsuccessfully to intercept the ball or intentionally knocks it down, the attacking team starts from a first-down Play the Ball.

13. The principle of advantage is applied.

14. A penalty is awarded for the following infringements: a forward pass, offside play, falsely claiming a touch, interfering with the Play the Ball (running around the ruck), and passing the ball once you have been touched. When a penalty is awarded, the referee advances the ball five meters from where the infringement occurred. The referee must give the exact mark from which the tap must be taken, and the defending team must retreat by five meters from that mark or behind the try line.

15. Repeated obstruction, excessive contact, verbal abuse, and foul play are not tolerated. The referee is the sole judge of these infractions. A penalty is awarded when these things occur, and a player can be given 2 minutes in the Sin Bin. Serious or continued foul play of any nature results in the player being ejected from the game without a replacement.

16. Play runs for 20 minutes with a 1-minute halftime. Repeat for up to three games, with 5 minutes rest between games.

CROSS-TRAINING

Cross-training for rugby players refers to forms of exercise that do not involve running. Valuable as supplements to a running-based fuel mix plan, cross-training options include

- cycling,
- swimming,
- rowing,
- step-machine exercises,
- climbing-machine exercises,
- aquatic jogging, and
- arm crank exercises.

Each of these modes of training improves general fuel mix conditioning and adds variety to a training program, a warm-up, or a rehabilitation plan. However, they should not dominate the fuel mix program because the movement patterns do not relate to rugby and therefore their effects are not specific.

Cross-training is also useful for heavy or aging players who need to reduce the amount of weight-bearing exercise or increase the amount of energy they expend to manage their body composition. Injured players also benefit from cross-training.

CROSS-TRAINING COMBO

Purpose: To improve general fuel mix conditioning. This drill uses cycling or rowing as an alternative to running-based training.

Equipment and area: Indoor cycle or rowing machine and a stopwatch.

Procedure: For this training session, you can use an indoor cycle, a rowing machine, or both by alternating intervals. Swimming, stepping, or working an arm crank device are also options.

1. Start the session by performing 4 continuous minutes of exercise and then resting for the period specified for your level of conditioning. For the second interval, cycle or row for 3 minutes, then rest, then continue, as set out in table 8.18, until you finish the set with 4 minutes of exercise.

2. Rest for the period indicated for your conditioning status and repeat for the specified number of sets. Players at the intermediate level of conditioning should stop after the fourth interval (one minute) of their second set.

3. Keep track of how far you travel during your 4-minute intervals to monitor your progress.

Key point: Apply the maximum training speed principle so that you travel about the same distance in your first and last intervals in a complete set.

Progression: Increase the period of rest between intervals by 30 seconds and raise your exercise intensity accordingly to encourage a greater contribution from anaerobic energy.

Table 8.18   Cross-Training Combo

Conditioning status	Intervals (min.)	Rest between intervals (min.:s.)	Sets	Rest between sets (min.:s.)
Basic	4-3-2-1-2-3-4	1:30	1	—
Intermediate	4-3-2-1-2-3-4	1:00	1.5	2:00
Advanced	4-3-2-1-2-3-4	0:45	2	2:00

RUGBY TRAINING

Rugby training emphasizes technical and tactical aspects of rugby. The conditioning benefits of rugby-training drills depend on the intensity, type, and volume of exercise.

It is worthwhile, particularly during the in-season, for the technical and conditioning coaches to work together closely to design training sessions that have a suitable conditioning benefit. Manipulating the work and rest times during sessions and drills to focus on aerobic, anaerobic, or fuel mix conditioning is one way to do this. The following sample strategies illustrate this point.

Rucking Drill

Doing repetitions of a technical rugby skill such as rucking at a high intensity for 25 seconds, followed by 2 minutes' rest, makes it more likely that you will perform at speeds close to or above those that occur during competition. This makes the drill specific and encourages dynamic rucking.

X, Y, or Z

Training sessions can be designated as X, Y, or Z based on the intensity of exercise. For example, a light team run undertaken the day before a competition would involve mostly jogging or striding during the rehearsal of team play patterns. This would not be taxing, and the main fuel supply would be aerobic, so the session would be designated an X.

A technical rugby session with work and rest times that mimic those typical in competition could be described as a Y. The energy supply would be mainly anaerobic, with some support from the aerobic system. Finally, a Z session would be a speed endurance conditioning session, because the work rate is very high and the rest times are long. Labeling and designing sessions using the X, Y, and Z method allows players and coaches to monitor training intensity and reduces the chances of over- or undertraining the energy systems. It also helps players prepare for training by letting them know what sort of session to expect!

> ## Dan's Top Tip

Rugby training is sometimes criticized as being "one paced" and for failing to meet or exceed match intensity. Vary your drill intensities by changing your recovery times between drills.

SAMPLE FUEL MIX PROGRAM

The following sample program, designed to improve fuel mix conditioning, progresses from general to specific fuel mix drills. The program includes three sessions per week, but if you are only able to perform two sessions, postpone the third session to the following week. The program may then be spread over nine weeks. Players with a poor level of fuel mix conditioning should repeat weeks 1 and 2 before progressing to weeks 3 to 6.

Six-Week Fuel Mix Program

Guidelines

- Base the volume and intensity of your session on your conditioning status. Guidelines are provided with each drill.
- Begin your warm-up with control and passing drills.
- Aim to have one day between sessions.

Week	Session 1	Session 2	Session 3
1	Three-Minute Intervals	Figure-Eight Intervals	Three-Minute Intervals
2	Figure-Eight Intervals	Pitch Line Circuit	Two-Minute Intervals (apply same set/rep/rest guidelines as per Three-Minute Intervals)
3	Pyramid Intervals	Pitch Line Circuit	Pyramid Intervals

(continued)

Week	Session 1	Session 2	Session 3
4	Running Clock Drill (maximum ball-in-play option) × 2 sets with 3 min. rest between sets	Lucky 13 Circuit	Running Clock Drill (pyramid option) × 2 sets with 3 min. rest between sets
5	Lucky 13 Circuit	Running Clock Drill (running fast scores tries option) × 2 sets with 3 min. rest	Lucky 13 Triangle Circuit
6	Team Agility Course 2 (chapter 7) × 10 laps with 90 s. rest between laps	Rest	Running Clock Drill—Specific Fuel Mix Test

CHAPTER 9

RECOVERY AND NUTRITION

Playing and training break you down, but recovery and nutrition build you back up. Recovery is now recognized as a training principle and an integral part of the training program. This chapter will help you formulate recovery strategies that will minimize fatigue and restore energy. It also covers guidelines on nutrition, including recommendations on nutrient and supplement intake and tips for gaining muscle mass and reducing body fat.

TRAINING STRESS

Fatigue is a direct effect and symptom of conditioning. Training stresses the energy stores (metabolism), nervous system, and mental toughness of players, which leads to improvements in complete conditioning. Training programs include recovery strategies because, by using them, the predictable and unavoidable stresses of training can be minimized and reversed.

Overtraining, on the other hand, is a result of excessive training with insufficient recovery, and it leads to a deterioration in performance. The negative effects of overtraining include low energy levels, chronic muscle soreness, increased resting pulse (also linked to poor sleep quality), sudden loss in body weight, illness or injury, lack of motivation, poor sleep quality, and poor appetite.

The challenge is to carefully plot and monitor the training plan and these symptoms so that the line between optimum training stress and overtraining is not crossed.

BENEFITS OF RECOVERY

The harder you train, the more important is the principle of recovery. Adhering to recovery strategies offers players three major benefits:

1. Effective adaptation to training. Optimizing recovery allows you to realize the improvements in conditioning that result from a progressive training program. Your recovery status influences the quality of and benefits received from each training session.

2. Resistance to injury and illness. Avoid your worst fear by adhering to the principle of recovery. Doing so allows you to reduce your risk of injury by ensuring that the muscles and supporting structures perform effectively and without inhibition. Proper training and recovery also support the immune system in its fight to keep illness at bay.

3. Ability to perform to your potential. Debilitating factors that prevent you from training and playing rugby to your potential include poor hydration status and insufficient energy stores. Optimizing recovery allows you to replenish the resources you need to play with greater consistency during training and competition.

RECOVERY STRATEGIES

Most international and professional rugby teams now use recovery strategies to optimize training and reduce the risk of overtraining and injury, and reduced muscle soreness, stiffness, lethargy, and reversibility are reportedly the result. You should experiment with the strategies in this chapter to determine what works best for you and your team.

Hydration

The first step in recovery is to replace fluids. During training and playing, the body controls its temperature by losing fluids, and failing to replace those fluids is a major problem. Excessive fluid loss reduces your endurance capacity, power, and concentration and increases reaction time. Losing more than 2 percent of your body weight is detrimental to performance and should be prevented by adhering to a fluid-intake plan in the pre- to postmatch period. Hyperhydrating—raising your body's fluid level above the normal rate—counteracts and reduces the negative effects of fluid loss during games and training.

A practical way to monitor sweat loss is to weigh yourself before and after exercise. Each pound of weight lost equals one pint of fluid, and each kilogram equals one and a half liters. These losses should be replaced as soon as possible by drinking water and sports drinks. Divide the total sweat loss by the duration of exercise for an estimate of the rate of loss, which can be used to predict fluid requirements.

Guidelines for Hydration

- Hyperhydrate before exercise.
- Drink fluids at regular intervals during training and competition.
- Use sports drinks to help replace electrolytes and energy.
- Avoid excessive amounts of caffeine and alcohol (they have a diuretic effect).
- Weigh yourself pre- and postexercise and calculate your rate of sweat loss.
- Monitor your urine color: It should be pale, not dark in color.

Stretching and Cooling Down

Performing static stretches after exercising promotes recovery. This cool-down effect, in combination with light aerobic exercise, helps remove such waste products as lactic acid and assists in returning muscles and joints to their normal length and mobility. This process allows the heart rate to slow to a resting pulse at a steady rate, reducing the pooling of blood in the legs. Including static stretching in a postexercise cool-down has also been shown to reduce the incidence of injuries by up to 50 percent in subsequent exercise sessions.

Incorporating dedicated flexibility sessions into your training program will also reduce stiffness, promote recovery, and correct body alignment. Returning your muscles and joints to their normal length and mobility allows the body to perform at its best. See chapter 5 for flexibility drills and routines.

Guidelines for Stretching and Cooling Down

- Include regular flexibility sessions in your program.
- Stretch to the point where you feel moderate tension, but not pain, in the muscle; pain results from the muscle trying to shorten.
- Spend extra time stretching chronically tight muscles.
- Drink fluids to rehydrate and eat snacks such as bananas to refuel during the stretching session.

Refueling

Sports drinks contain carbohydrates and boost energy levels during exercise. Teams should drink them during the game and at halftime to help them endure the full 80 minutes of play. A banana eaten at halftime is a useful source of energy and also helps to prevent muscle cramping.

After a hard session or match, fruits, sandwiches, and protein shakes start the refueling process. A meal containing a protein source and a combination of carbohydrates should be eaten within an hour of finishing a game or training session. More information on refueling appears later in this chapter.

Water-Based Strategies

Research studies have shown that using water to promote recovery reduces fatigue and inflammation and speeds the clearance of lactic acid from the muscles. These strategies include contrast showers, an ice bath, and exercising in a swimming pool.

Contrast Showers

Take contrast showers after exercising throughout the week, and perhaps even as a morning ritual.

Shortly after exercising, alternate between 1-minute warm showers and 1-minute cold showers for 8 to 10 minutes. The contrast in temperature promotes blood flow and stimulates the nervous system, both of which positively influence recovery and arousal levels.

Ice Bath

The ice bath is an appropriate postmatch or contact training strategy because it has a more significant cooling effect than a cold shower does. This reduces inflammation caused by contact and requires very little effort on the part of the player.

Method: Fill a bathtub with cold water and several kilograms of ice cubes so that the water is 10 to 15 degrees C. Spend between 30 seconds and 3 minutes in the bath (closer to 3 minutes for high-contact players, such as the five front-row forwards). Separate four to six intervals in the ice bath with 1 or 2 minutes in a warm shower or spa.

Active Pool Session

An active pool session, like the ice bath and contrast showers, promotes recovery by stimulating blood flow. The pool-based movements, including swimming, jogging, and functional stretching, also promote muscle and joint flexibility.

In water one meter deep, walk, lunge, and swim in intervals separated by static stretching. Your movements should be slow and aerobic and incorporate multidirectional lunges and arm movements through the water. The session, lasting no more than 15 to 20 minutes, should not be taxing. Aquatic jogging is also an option.

Massage

Sports massage relaxes muscles, reduces the feeling of fatigue, and stimulates blood flow. Like an active pool session, massage helps muscles and joints return to their normal length, but it is the better method of the two when you are very tired because you don't have to expend any energy.

Self-massage also helps players to identify tense muscles. Get in the habit of feeling tight muscle groups and relieving the tension with your hands or a small ball. The foam roller, described in chapter 5, can also be used for self-massage, as shown in figure 9.1.

"Regen" Session

The "regen" (regeneration) or resetting session is a next-day recovery workout that includes a series of light aerobic exercises and balance, control, and static core stabilization drills to help restore the balance of tension and mobility to the body. Dan uses the regen session shown in table 9.1 the day after a match.

Figure 9.1 A foam roller can be used for self-massage.

Table 9.1 Dan's Twenty-Minute Pool Regen Session

Activity	Interval
Deepwater aquatic jogging	5 min.
Single-leg balancing in shallow (1 m) water	5 repetitions of 10 s. on each leg
Swimming (various strokes)	2 repetitions of 25 m
Multidirectional lunging in shallow (1 m) water	3 repetitions of 30 s. with 15 s. of rest between repetitions
Static stretching	2 min.
Squat rotations: Bend your knees, join your hands together with arms straight, and rotate clockwise then counterclockwise with your hands in the water before straightening your legs. Repeat.	2 sets of 10 repetitions (a squat followed by a rotation in each direction equals 1 repetition), resting for 20 s. between sets
Shallow-water (1 m) aquatic jogging	2 sets of 45 s. with 15 s. of rest between sets
Static stretching and drinking fluids	2 min.

Rest Management

Players and coaches need to be aware of the different types of rest that players need.

Interset Rest

The amount of rest time between, for example, speed and agility drills, must be adequate so that players' performance quality remains high in successive efforts. During fuel mix conditioning, the rest time between intervals of exercise dictates the level of recovery and the subsequent contributions of the anaerobic and aerobic energy systems. For example, three repetitions of a 400-meter run with four minutes for recovery would use mostly anaerobic energy, whereas a one-minute interset recovery would require a greater contribution from the aerobic system.

More details on the appropriate rest times between fuel mix, speed, agility, strength, and power drills are given in the discussions on those components of conditioning.

Tapering

Tapering the training program means reducing the training volume, intensity, or both before a specific event or phase. In the in-season, training must be tapered so that players can recover in time to be fresh for competition. The in-season training week must include at least one recovery day.

Passive Rest

On recovery days and during rest phases throughout the year, passive rest is not necessarily the best option. During the in-season, doing no exercise at all is a negative shock to a professional player's system. Instead, rest should be active, including, for example, light aerobic exercise (in the pool, cycling, or rowing, for example) or a light resistance session using light dumbbells and body weight movements, to recruit but not fatigue muscles. Control and static core stabilization drills may also be used as active rest exercises.

Periodization

Long-term planning called *periodization* is the division of the season's training plan into phases or cycles. Following the final game of the season, players should begin an active rest phase of several weeks of light exercise to recover physically and mentally but minimize the loss in general conditioning. Similarly, phases of training during the in-season must also include active rest phases so that players' and coaches' energy levels and attitudes can be refreshed. More information about the training principle of periodization can be found in chapter 2.

Sleep, Stress, and Relaxation

High-quality sleep recharges your muscles and nervous system. Try to stick to a routine to get a regular amount of sleep. Relaxation helps you to achieve a regular sleep pattern and combat stress. Sleep experts recommend going to sleep at the same time each night and waking up naturally, whenever possible.

Excessive stress slows down the recovery process and weakens the immune system. The muscular tension caused by stress is wasted energy and reduces flexibility and coordination. Strategies such as positive self-talk and relaxation drills help to reduce stress by preventing negative thoughts and images.

Figure 9.2 Recovery pants help alleviate blood pooling.

Guidelines for Sleep and Relaxation

- Avoid caffeine and large meals before bedtime.
- Try to get at least eight hours' sleep every night.
- Power nap during the day if you have trained hard.
- Listen to relaxing music before bed and then turn it off at bedtime.
- Wake up at least three hours before training.
- Consult with a sport psychologist about strategies for relaxation and positive self-talk.

Recovery Pants

After training or playing, a large volume of blood and lactic acid may pool in your legs. Called *blood pooling*, it can be reduced by stretching and cooling down correctly. To support tired muscles and encourage blood to flow back to the heart after exercising, players may also consider wearing recovery pants, like the ones shown in figure 9.2.

These body-molded pants mildly compress the muscles of the lower body, supporting body alignment and blood flow.

Alcohol

Rugby players are notorious for indulging in alcohol after matches, but it interferes with the recovery process in a number of ways. Alcohol hampers not only hydration and energy replenishment, but also the repair of tissue damaged by contact. The standard medical treatment for damaged tissues—rest, ice, compression, and elevation—constricts the vessels surrounding the injury to reduce swelling and inflammation. Alcohol, however, dilates vessels, which may lead to swelling, which impedes the repair process.

If you must drink alcohol after exercising, drink a half-pint of water for every pint of beer to help minimize alcohol's diuretic effect, and make sure food is also part of the party!

Monitoring Recovery Status

People have different rates of recovery because of their unique physiology and playing position, and training for both the individual and the team must be adapted accordingly. For example, front-row forwards use more energy and undergo more contact than outside backs, so they will probably experience a greater degree of postmatch fatigue. The training plan must take this and other individual variables into consideration.

Subjective Monitoring

Subjective monitoring can be used to assess recovery status. Players can use a daily monitoring sheet like the one in table 9.2 to assess the factors that determine individual recovery status.

An individual training diary is an excellent tool for monitoring recovery factors and measures such as resting heart rate and fluid and food intake. Performance measures should also be documented in the diary, including details of the loads lifted during strength and power sessions, and also used to gauge recovery. For example, if a player typically lifts 100 kilograms for three repetitions during an explosive lifting session but in the scheduled lifting session struggles to lift 90 kilograms, then it is likely that the player's metabolism or nervous system probably has not fully recovered. Instead of continuing with the explosive lifting workout, the player should switch to either active rest or an alternative training session, such as a light strength-based lifting session. This alternative session does not stress the metabolism or nervous system in

Table 9.2 Recovery Monitoring Sheet

Factor	Rating				
Energy level	1	2	3	4	5
Quality of sleep	1	2	3	4	5
Self-confidence and self-esteem	1	2	3	4	5
Muscle soreness	1	2	3	4	5
Motivation and enthusiasm for training	1	2	3	4	5
Attitude toward training	1	2	3	4	5
Health	1	2	3	4	5

1 = awful; 2 = poor; 3 = OK; 4 = good; 5 = excellent
Adapted from Angela Calder, 2002 *Recovery Training Workbook*, NCF.

the same way as explosive lifting does, but it still allows the player to perform a worthwhile training session.

NUTRITION

Optimizing nutrition leads to better health and higher standards of performance. This section addresses and provides guidelines for the key topics concerning a nutrition plan: fuel for performance, the importance of protein, good and bad fats, supplements, and pre- and postmatch food intake.

Fuel for Performance

To meet the demands of training and competing, players require food that can be broken down into usable energy. Carbohydrates are the most appropriate sources of fuel for rugby players, and they should form the bulk of caloric intake. Foods such as rice, pasta, potatoes, and bread are rich in carbohydrates and are broken down into glycogen (which produces energy) and distributed throughout the body to be used when exercising.

Intensive training and competing place heavy demands on glycogen stores. As these stores are depleted, fatigue occurs and performance drops until players "hit the wall" and run out entirely. Players can avoid emptying their glycogen tank by basing their carbohydrate intake on their body weight and activity level. Table 9.3 shows the formula for estimating the daily carbohydrate requirement based on a player's body weight and training volume.

The different types of carbohydrates vary in their rates of absorption, digestion, and influence on blood sugar levels. A food's glycemic index (GI) is used to describe the rate at which the food raises blood glucose levels. High-GI foods, such as white bread and honey, rapidly increase blood sugar and trigger the production of large amounts of insulin to counteract the rise. Low-GI carbohydrates, such as apples, porridge, oats, and lentils, have a slower rate of sugar absorption and therefore produce less insulin. Low-GI, carbohydrate-rich foods are more appropriate sources of energy for fueling training and competition, and they reduce the likelihood of carbohydrate intake increasing body fat amounts. High-GI foods are beneficial immediately after exercise because they help the blood sugar quickly return to a normal level.

Table 9.3   Estimated Carbohydrate Requirement Based on Body Weight and Training Program

Weekly training program summary	Suggested daily carbohydrate intake (per kg body weight)
2 sessions rugby training (90 min.) and 1 match	5-7 g
2 sessions rugby training, 2 sessions strength training, 1 session speed drills, 1 session fuel mix conditioning, and 1 match	8-10 g
Off-season recovery phase: one 30 min. cycling session, one 20 min. swim, one 45 min. tennis session	4-5 g

Guidelines for Fueling

- Match your energy intake (in the form of food) with your body weight and training demands.

- Emphasize low-GI, carbohydrate-rich foods rather than high-GI foods in your normal diet.

- Eat high-GI foods—bananas, sports drinks, pasta, for example—immediately after exercising.

- Eat fewer refined and simple carbohydrates, such as white bread and sugar.

- Eat smaller meals and eat more often to encourage stable energy and blood sugar levels.
- Eat complex carbohydrates three hours before a competition or hard training session.
- Eat as much variety as possible. Instead of focusing on wheat-based products—such as cereals, breads, and snack bars—try rye bread, oats, or quinoa flakes instead.

Protein

Rugby players require a greater intake of protein than sedentary people do because protein builds muscle and helps to repair muscle damaged during contact or weight training. Protein is also an energy source, although that is not its primary role. It can be burned as a backup fuel to produce energy when glycogen levels are in short supply—like the crucial last 10 minutes of a tough game.

Similar to that for carbohydrates, protein intake should be regulated according to body weight and the amounts of strength, power, and contact training in the program. Players who want to increase or maintain muscle mass while following a demanding conditioning program require up to 2.2 grams of protein per kilogram of body weight in their diet each day. Because it's difficult to take in enough meat, dairy products, and other protein-rich foods to meet that requirement in a day, many players use protein drinks (whey protein powder mixed with nonfat or low-fat milk or water) to help them reach this level of intake.

Guidelines for Protein Intake

- Include a protein source in most of your meals.
- Use a wide variety of protein sources, such as eggs, fish, chicken, nuts, peas, and beans.
- Beware of the fat content of your protein source.
- Boost your protein intake with a protein drink, if necessary. (Note: Professional and international players are now warned against taking protein shakes unless every batch of supplements is tested for contamination of illegal substances. You may also consider making your own protein shakes with skimmed milk powder.)

Fat

Not all fats are equal. Whereas saturated fat is unhealthy and implicated in heart disease, polyunsaturated fats play an important role in supporting health and performance by boosting the immune system, building cells, and providing energy for low-intensity exercise and normal daily activities. The fat content in your diet should range from 20 to 30 percent of your total caloric intake, which is less than the amount consumed by the average person.

Players who consistently expend a lot of energy and have an optimum level of body fat do not need to be as concerned about fat intake as players with excessive body fat or low energy output. All players should avoid eating fatty foods both before and immediately after training because it may slow the absorption of carbohydrates and proteins.

Guidelines for Fat Intake

- Avoid saturated fats, such as visible fat on meat, butter, and lard, and trans fats such as margarine and deep-fried foods. Diets high in saturated fats and trans fats increase low-density lipoprotein (LDL) or "bad" cholesterol levels and, therefore, the risk of heart disease, whereas most unsaturated fats have harmless or even helpful effects on one's lipid profile.
- Eat fish two or three times a week to boost your intake of essential fish oils.
- Use olive oil for cooking and in salad dressings.
- Avoid eating fatty foods prior to and following exercise.

Reducing Your Body Fat Percentage

The higher the level of rugby play, the lower the percentage of players' body fat. Top male players' body composition is typically 8 to 12 percent fat, in contrast to the general population's average of over 16 percent. International female players aim for a level of about 20 percent, compared to almost 30 percent for the average nonathlete.

The most appropriate and effective method of reducing body fat is to manipulate food intake and energy expenditure. Players with excessive body fat should slowly reduce their total caloric intake so that it falls short of their energy expenditure (that amount needed for metabolism, growth, and exercise), thus creating a negative energy balance. They can also add to their training program low-intensity cross-training drills that use fat as an energy source.

Guidelines for Reducing Body Fat

- Reduce your fat intake to 15 to 20 percent of your total caloric intake.
- Include several short cross-training fuel mix sessions in your program; a 25-minute cycling session in the morning and evening is better that just one 60-minute session at lunchtime.

- Do not crash diet! This is not healthy and will cause you to lose muscle and energy that you need for training and playing.
- Aim for a one- to two-pound (one-half to one kilogram) reduction in body fat per week, and set realistic short- and long-term goals.
- Manage your blood sugar level by avoiding large quantities of carbohydrates in one sitting and reducing the amount of food with a high glycemic index in your diet.

Building Muscle Mass

Rugby is a high-intensity collision sport, so players need good muscle size, strength, and power. Statistics show that players are getting heavier and more muscular, and in general this trend is not compromising their mobility on the pitch. However, players should be careful not to become obsessed with gaining muscle mass; many players of below-average body weight have excelled in rugby by optimizing speed, agility, and fuel mix conditioning in their training programs.

Players who focus too much on size also tend to neglect other elements of their conditioning. Some players actually reduce their power and mobility if their increases in size have not led to increases in functional strength. Ensure that your body-weight goals are appropriate by taking into account your playing position, body type, and overall level of conditioning.

Guidelines for Increasing Muscle Mass

- Ensure that your caloric intake exceeds your caloric expenditure.
- Focus on gaining muscle mass during the off-season.
- Gradually increase your protein intake up to 2.2 grams per kilogram of body weight.
- Include periodic phases of hypertrophy strength training (not all year long!), but do not neglect functional drills. Refer to table 6.1 on page 75 in chapter 6 for more information on hypertrophy strength training.

Pre- and Postmatch Diet

Increase your carbohydrate intake and taper your training during the two days prior to a game. Your goal is to encourage your muscles to store glycogen so they are prepared for playing high-energy rugby. On the day of the match, eat your main meal about three and a half hours before kickoff. Eat primarily complex carbohydrates and small amounts of protein, and avoid fatty foods and red meat because they require too much blood to be brought to the stomach for digestion. If you are hungry within an hour of competition, eat a small apple or banana.

Dan's Prematch Meal Routine

If kickoff is at 2 P.M., I eat breakfast at about 9 A.M., which consists of poached eggs, toast, and tomatoes. Lunch, at about 12 P.M., consists of spaghetti and baked beans (for plenty of carbohydrates). Unlike some players, I can eat two hours before kickoff and digest the meal in time to play. I stick to the "eat little, but often" rule during the rest of the week, so I never eat large portions. I also have a meal-replacement drink with me in case I feel hungry before the kickoff.

Postmatch, your first priority is to drink fluids. Rehydration should start during the game and at halftime by regularly sipping water or a sports drink, and you must continue hydrating after the game, before you eat. After the match is the ideal time to eat high-GI foods to boost blood sugar levels and start refueling the muscles. A protein shake and carbohydrates in the forms of fruit (bananas and grapes, for example), sandwiches, and muffins are good to start with, and then follow with a main meal within an hour of finishing the game. Eat a snack every hour postmatch for up to six hours.

Guidelines for Pre- and Postmatch Food Intake

- Eat a main meal consisting of complex-carbohydrate-rich foods and a small protein source at least three hours prior to kickoff.
- Have a small snack such as an apple an hour before kickoff if you feel hungry.
- Avoid large amounts of protein and fatty foods, such as chicken, french fries, and steak.
- Drink plenty of fluids.
- Experiment with foods during training to find what best serves your energy needs and tastes.
- Maintain a high caloric intake (mainly carbohydrates and protein) the day after a game.

Supplements

Several supplementary aids, such as creatine and isotonic sports drinks, have been proven to enhance performance in specific elements of rugby fitness. However, many products make misleading promises, so you should ask the following questions before using a supplement:

- Is the substance banned by the International Olympic Committee?
- Are there any short- or long-term side effects to usage?
- Is there scientific support for the supplement's purported benefits?
- Who recommended the product to you?

Dedication to a sound nutritional plan and a well-designed training regimen are your primary means of meeting your energy requirements. However, players whose positions demand very high levels of energy will probably benefit from boosting their nutrient intake with protein shakes and meal-replacement drinks. The following are supplements that elite rugby players regularly use:

- Protein powder to boost protein intake
- Creatine to support recovery from anaerobic training
- BCAA, branch chained amino acids, for building muscle
- Caffeine, although it is illegal over a certain limit
- Glutamine to boost the immune system and prevent the breakdown of muscle
- Glucosamine and cod liver oil to support the building and repair of cartilage and other supporting structures
- Vitamins and minerals, the need for which should be met by a well-balanced diet, but you may want to add them as a supplement if your diet is poor and your training levels are high

SUMMARY

Recovery strategies, including the management of nutrition, are of growing importance as players search for ways to get that extra edge in complete conditioning. Players should be encouraged to monitor their recovery status and to use the various strategies that promote recovery. Coaches must also plan their training programs to take into account the differences in individuals' recovery rates and include regular recovery periods during the rugby year.

CHAPTER 10

COMPLETE RUGBY TRAINING PROGRAMS

A systematic, step-by-step approach is needed to formulate an individual training program. This approach—explained in the preceding chapters of this book—considers the demands of the sport, the individual player, training principles, and sport-specific drills and training systems. Once the program has been designed and training is under way, the player's conditioning is monitored by detailing in a training diary the contents and results of training sessions and evaluating progress with periodic fitness testing. See table 10.1 for a summary of the process and the chapters to refer to for more information.

In this chapter, we will review these steps and describe how to select and integrate the drills and strategies detailed in *Complete Conditioning for Rugby*. We will also look at the principles and some examples of reconditioning after injury and some sample in- and off-season programs for amateur and professional rugby players.

Table 10.1 Systematic Six-Step Plan for Designing a Training Program

Step number	Design focus	Chapter for reference
1	Analyze the conditioning demands of the sport.	1
2	Evaluate the player's training and fitness status and set realistic conditioning goals.	3
3	Adhere to proven training principles.	2
4	Review and select drills that develop the elements of conditioning essential to preventing injury and enhancing performance.	4-8
5	Design and apply the training program.	10
6	Monitor and evaluate the player's progress.	3 and 9

STEP 1: CONDITIONING DEMANDS OF RUGBY

The facts and figures in chapter 1 highlight the conditioning demands of competitive rugby. This information supports the need for a varied training program that integrates elements of strength, power, speed, agility, and fuel mix conditioning.

- Rugby players require high levels of stability, strength, and power to reduce the likelihood of injury resulting from contact situations and to perform the specific movement patterns of competition, including tackling, being tackled, rucking, and mauling.

- Players need to develop speed and agility to run at high speeds, sprint at maximal speed, and execute quick changes in direction.

- Players rely heavily on fuel mix conditioning to enable them to repeat and effectively recover from movement patterns.

- Players require a multitude of positional motor skills, including those involved in passing, catching, kicking, and scrummaging.

Because each position places unique demands on the player, training programs that are position-specific must be developed.

STEP 2: PLAYER PROFILE AND TRAINING GOALS

Testing, evaluating, and goal setting are integral parts of a conditioning program. A formal fitness test should be performed at the beginning of a training program or phase and repeated periodically. This testing measures all elements of conditioning, providing essential feedback for target setting and the basis for program design. Examples of tests and standards are in chapter 3. Typical training goals include

- increase strength and power for acceleration speed improvement,
- improve core stability and flexibility for correcting posture,
- reduce body fat by altering the diet and performing fuel mix drills, and
- increase muscle mass and strength for contact by using pattern and loaded strength drills.

STEP 3: TRAINING PRINCIPLES

Training principles are essential components of a systematic approach to conditioning and increase the safety and effectiveness of training. Covered in detail in chapters 2 and 9, they include

- injury prevention,
- specificity,
- overload,
- periodization,
- recovery, and
- enjoyment.

The most important of these principles is injury prevention, which encourages players and coaches to adhere to certain principles when performing and selecting training drills. An injury prevention strategy for safe and progressive overload should adhere to these guidelines:

- Simple to complex
- Stable to unstable

- Body weight to extra resistance
- Low load to high load

STEP 4: CONDITIONING DRILLS AND SYSTEMS

A complete conditioning program includes drills representing all the components of conditioning. These drills are apportioned in relation to the playing position and conditioning profile of the player.

The battery of drills listed in *Complete Conditioning for Rugby* presents players and coaches with a path for progression and adds variety to the training program. The following guidelines explain the appropriate methods of progression for selecting training drills.

Selecting Strength and Power Drills

Players and coaches should progress from core stabilization drills to loaded strength and power drills. Figure 6.1 illustrates this pyramid of strength and power training drills (see page 72).

Programs should always begin with a phase of movement strength drills before introducing loads or speed to movements. Players who have progressed to power drills need to preserve and continue to enhance their level of movement strength by still including some of these drills in their training program. These drills can be performed in a separate training session, as a warm-up routine, or in a superset with loaded or power training drills.

Players between the ages of 16 and 18 should focus on body-weight drills (control, core stabilization, and pattern strength drills) as well as on developing correct technique for loaded and explosive lifting drills. Loaded strength drills should be introduced gradually with loads that are light enough to allow a minimum of 10 repetitions.

Selecting Fuel Mix Conditioning Drills

When training to develop their fuel mix conditioning, players and teams both benefit from combining general and specific fuel mix drills. The same is true for off-season training, which has traditionally focused exclusively on general fuel mix drills. Combining the two types ensures that the energy system pathways continue to be familiar with the fuel demands of competitive rugby. During the in-season phase, players should reduce their volume of fuel mix conditioning to allow optimum recovery for competition.

> ### Dan's Top Tip

As a full-time rugby player who is in reasonable cardio-vascular condition, I tend not to need any aerobic training. Intense anaerobic sessions and general rugby training are enough to keep me aerobically conditioned. However, if you are coming back from injury, have too much body fat, or sit in an office all day, it is unwise to try to build specific fuel mix conditioning and speed on a weak aerobic base. Develop your aerobic system first, with general fuel mix drills.

Players who exhibit poor levels of fuel mix fitness in the Running Clock Drill or Three-Kilometer Run should focus on general fuel mix drills during the early stages of their program, but also incorporate specific drills such as Grid Tag and Touch Rugby. Cross-training drills also boost fuel mix fitness, but they should not be the focus of the training program.

The higher work rate required of forwards compared to backs during competitive rugby (caused by the higher volume of tackles, rucks, and set piece plays that forwards participate in) highlights the greater fuel mix conditioning demands placed on props, hookers, and second- and back-row forwards. In the training program, therefore, forwards need to per-form a greater percentage of fuel mix drills than backs do. Similarly, inside backs require higher levels of fuel mix fitness than do outside backs.

The intensity and volume of fuel mix training drills in a training session depend largely on the individual's level of fuel mix condition-ing. The better the level of fuel mix fitness, the greater should be the intensity and volume of fuel mix drills. Table 8.1 identifies three catego-ries into which players can be divided based on their training age and performance on a fuel mix fitness test (see page 187). These categories—basic, intermediate, and advanced—dictate the number and length of the rest periods permitted during the fuel mix drills in chapter 8.

Selecting Speed and Agility Drills

The conditioning program must always include speed and agility training because these qualities rely heavily on the memory of the nervous system. If these drills are neglected, the body starts to forget how to move and change direction quickly.

The drills in chapter 7 (Speed and Agility Drills) fall into four categories:

1. Acceleration speed
2. Basic speed
3. Programmed agility drills
4. Reactive agility drills

All players should focus on acceleration drills in the training program. Outside backs should also incorporate basic speed drills. For agility, progress from programmed to reactive agility drills.

Integrating Training Objectives

To most effectively encourage adaptation to training, focus on the specific elements of conditioning that are emphasized in the training phase as you also minimize the loss of conditioning of other elements. There are phases in the competitive season when a general mix of training is called for, but training blocks, which usually range from three to six weeks in length, divide the year into periods that have a theme. An effective training block combines, for example, speed and strength, or fuel mix conditioning and strength endurance. You should not combine speed and endurance components because the latter fatigues players, inhibiting effective speed development.

STEP 5: TRAINING PROGRAMS

Table 2.1 shows how the training year is divided into four phases (see page 18): active rest, off-season, preseason, and in-season. The training plan during these periods should emphasize particular training drills and objectives. Follow this table's recommendations when designing your training program's content.

Sample Programs

Table 10.2 shows training programs for well-conditioned amateur and professional rugby players. The table illustrates the integration of rugby

Table 10.2   Sample In-Season Training Program for Professional and Amateur Rugby Players

Session	Professional players		Amateur players	
	Morning	Afternoon	Morning	Evening
Monday	Strength 1	Skills and FM1		Strength 1
Tuesday	Speed and Agility and rugby training	Strength 2		Rugby training and FM1
Wednesday	Power 1 and rugby training	Injury Prevention		Power 1
Thursday	Rest	Flexibility		Speed and Agility and rugby training
Friday	Team Run		Rest	Rest
Saturday	Power-Up	Match	Match	
Sunday	Regen		Regen	

training, competition, and conditioning during an in-season phase of the training plan. See table 10.3 for the drills to include in the workouts identified in table 10.2.

The contents of these training sessions are shown in table 10.3. Because professional players are likely to have a superior level of conditioning and more time to spend training, the professional program includes more training volume, types, and intensity.

Individualized Programs

The off-season sample programs are designed for three players who have different conditioning profiles and training targets. The players' characteristics are summarized in table 10.4, and their profiles and targets are given in table 10.5. Compared to the in-season program, off-season training uses a higher percentage and volume of conditioning and does not taper for competition. See tables 10.6 and 10.7 for the programs.

Table 10.3　Session Content for Professional and Amateur Training Programs

Training session	Professional players	Amateur players
Strength 1	• Warm-up: control drills and skipping	
	• Back Squat, 4 sets of 4 repetitions each, rest 3 min. between sets	
	• Deadlift, 4 sets of 3 repetitions each, rest 3 min. between sets	
	• Hamstring Pendulum, 3 sets of 6 repetitions each, rest 2 min. between sets	
	• Weighted Push-Up, 4 sets of 4 repetitions each, rest 2 min. between sets	
	• Weighted Supine Maul-Up, 4 sets of 6 repetitions each, rest 2 min. between sets	
	• Core stabilization medley, 15 min.	
	• Static stretching	
	• Ice bath (postsession)	
FM1	Specific fuel mix conditioning: Running Clock Drill, 10 repetitions, rest 2 min. between repetitions	Specific fuel mix conditioning: Touch Rugby, 20 min., 2 min. halftime, after rugby training
Speed and Agility	• Top-Five Ladder Drills, 2 repetitions of each drill	• Top-Five Ladder Drills, 2 repetitions of each drill
	• Eyes Wide Shut, 4 repetitions of 15 s. each on each leg	• Hollow Sprints, 4 repetitions, full recovery between repetitions
	• Body Lean Accelerations, 4 repetitions	
	• Hollow Sprints, 2 repetitions, full recovery between repetitions	
	• Medicine Ball Chuck and Chase, 2 repetitions, full recovery between repetitions	

Training session	Professional players	Amateur players
Strength 2	• Push-Up and Pull with weighted vest, 5 sets of 4 repetitions, superset with Shoulder Step-Up with weighted vest, 8 repetitions, 1 min. rest between sets • Multichop with medicine ball, 3 sets of 16 repetitions each • Prone Extensions, 4 sets of 20 repetitions, rest 30 s. between sets	
Power 1	Explosive lifts: • Power Clean, superset of 3 sets of 4 repetitions with 2 repetitions of single-leg Positive Hops on each leg, rest 4 min. between sets • Hang Split Snatch, 4 sets of 3 repetitions, rest 3 min. between sets	Explosive lifts: • Hang Clean, superset of 3 sets of 4 repetitions with 4 repetitions of Jump and Fix (3 mini hurdles), rest 4 min. between sets • Push Press (standing shoulder press with assistance from legs), superset of 3 sets of 4 repetitions each with 2 repetitions of 5 m sprint starts (sprint 5 m from a crouched start position), rest 3 min. between sets.
Injury Prevention	• Physiotherapist-supervised circuit of control and core stabilization drills and shoulder stabilization drills with a resistance band	

(continued)

Table 10.3 *(continued)*

Training session	Professional players	Amateur players
Power-Up	• Top-Five Ladder Drills, 1 repetition of each drill • Single-Leg Bridge, 4 repetitions of 10 s. each on each leg • Rotating Ramp, 4 repetitions • Power Clean, 4 sets of 2 repetitions at 40% of 1RM, rest 3 min. between sets • Total session time = 20 min.	
Regen	• Aquatic jogging, 10 min.; slow swimming, 2 lengths; pattern drills in 1 m water: Lunge and Dummy Pass, 10 to each side; Multi-directional Lunge, 5 repetitions; Multichop, pushing rugby ball through water, 10 repetitions on each side • Static stretch, 10 min. • Finish with contrast showers	• Cycling, 20 min. • Static and self-release stretches, 15 min.
Flexibility	• Cycling, 10 min. • Medley of static, active, and self-release stretches, 30 min.	

Player Profiles

Test Case 1. I've always played prop due to my natural size and strength. At school, I was very good at explosive events like shot put and discus, but always suffered on the cross-country runs! My test scores confirm my obvious weaknesses but provide a benchmark for setting targets, and I know I have the motivation to reach and exceed my goals. I have just started training full-time as an Academy professional so I can dedicate all my time to training.

Test Case 2. I'm 21 and in my final year at a university, training to be a PE teacher. Having played loads of sports up to the county level, including hockey, swimming, and athletics, I took up rugby at the university and now play on the wing for my club. I've got good natural pace, but I haven't done much rugby-specific speed and agility, and I still need to work on my strength and power, because I've not lifted weights that often. Although my teacher training takes up most of my time, I'm happy to commit myself to three or four training sessions per week to develop my conditioning.

Test Case 3. I started my playing career as a back-row forward and represented my country at the U19 level. I'm now 19, and although I'm faster and fitter than most players, I'm smaller than the average back-row forward and my coach recommends that I change my position to scrum-half. This is probably my best option because I aspire to represent my country at senior level, but I'm afraid my size will hold me back. I'm studying sport science at the university, so I've got a good understanding of conditioning principles and I'll be able to train almost every day until exams. I've lifted weights for several years because my PE teacher was a qualified weightlifting coach, so my lifting technique is fine.

Player Fitness Test Results and Targets

Table 10.5 details the current fitness status of these players and their medium-term (12-week) targets for each element of conditioning.

Designing Your Program

The contents of the sample programs are clearly different for each player, and specific to their training targets and objectives. If your training goals match or are similar to one of the sample programs, you can adopt the sample as your program, modifying it where necessary. If your aim, like test case 3, is to gain size and strength and your fuel mix conditioning is also a weakness, follow a six-week strength-based program similar to that presented for test case 3, and then increase the percentage of fuel mix drills in your next phase of training.

The secret to reaching your individual targets is good planning; do not try to develop every element of conditioning in the same training phase! Set goals for the long-term and plan, for example, three six-week programs, each having a different emphasis. Also ensure that the programs help you to maintain other elements of conditioning even while they emphasize a specific area for progression.

Table 10.4 Test Cases

	Test case 1	Test case 2	Test case 3
Age	20	21	19
Gender	Male	Female	Male
Position	Tight head prop	Wing	Scrum-half
Conditioning strengths	• Strength • Speed and agility	• Low body fat • Fuel mix conditioning	• Fuel mix conditioning • Speed and agility
Conditioning weaknesses	• High body fat • Fuel mix conditioning	• Acceleration speed and agility • Core stability • Strength and power	• Strength and power • Size
8-week program summary	• Focus on general and specific fuel mix drills • Reduce caloric intake • Maintain levels of strength and speed	• Focus on speed and agility drills • Develop foundation movement strength • Progress to loaded strength drills	• Increase caloric intake • Focus on loaded strength drills • Maintain speed, agility, and fuel mix conditioning

(continued)

Table 10.4 *(continued)*

	Test case 1	Test case 2	Test case 3
Program design notes	• Gradually reduce intake of high-glycemic carbohydrates; significant reduction in caloric intake is not required because the new training program significantly increases energy expenditure • Cross-training session to lessen load on joints, reducing likelihood of repetitive impact injuries • Speed and Agility session planned for Thursday so that your legs are fresh for it • Go for a 20 min. fast walk or medium-pace cycle at least twice per week from week 4	• Follow a 4-week dedicated core stabilization program to develop a foundation for pattern and loaded strength drills • Focus on pattern strength drills before increasing volume of loaded strength drills so that your body has time to adapt • Wednesday is a free day at the university, so there will be A.M. and P.M. sessions • Core stabilization medley includes a selection of drills covered during the 4-week core stabilization program to maintain progress • FM1 changes to Speed and Agility 2 because your fuel mix fitness is strong and can be maintained with only rugby training	• Speed and Agility session planned for Thursday so that your legs are fresh • Eat snacks, such as a peanut butter sandwich, between main meals and have a protein shake in the morning and before going to bed • Because you are changing positions, strongly emphasize positional skills during your warm-up routines • Upper-body sessions to be split into pulling and pushing so that muscles can be overloaded with 8-12 sets in the same session and because you can then lift upper-body weights on consecutive days • Progress to explosive lifts in next program

Table 10.5   Test Case Fitness Profiles and Targets

Test	Test case 1 (prop)		Test case 2 (center)		Test case 3 (scrum-half)	
	Result	Target	Result	Target	Result	Target
Body mass (kg)	120	117	75	75	73	80
Body fat (%)	23	18	20	20	10	10
Running Clock Drill (s.)	305	260	250	240	210	210
10 m Sprint (s.)	1.95	1.93	2.33	2.24	1.94	1.89
30 m Sprint (s.)	4.27	4.22	4.65	4.45	4.24	4.19
T Test (s.)	10.9	10.6	13.5	12.0	9.8	9.5
Side Ramp (s.)	65	80	35	60	75	80
Bench Press 3RM (kg)	125	130	50	63	90	100
Vertical Jump Test (cm)	37	39	28	34	39	44

STEP 6: MONITORING AND EVALUATING

Evaluation is an ongoing part of the training process. Players and coaches should record the details of each conditioning and rugby session in their training diary, documenting the drills, loads, sets, and repetitions performed as well as the rest times. Reviewing the diary will provide feedback on performance and progression.

Objective and subjective measures should also be used regularly to assess a player's physical and mental status. A battery of fitness tests should be performed at least three times per year, and specific tests that measure elements in need of improvement can be administered every six to eight weeks. These test results can be used to update targets, monitor reconditioning following injury, and revise the training program. Some of these monitoring measures are discussed in the chapters on Rugby Fitness Testing (chapter 3) and Recovery and Nutrition (chapter 9).

The ultimate test of complete conditioning is, of course, your performance during competition, including your success in avoiding preventable injuries. Feeling strong and fast over 80 minutes of rugby play is the best type of conditioning feedback there is.

Table 10.6 Six-Week Individual Off-Season Training Program

	Test case 1		Test case 2		Test case 3	
	Morning	Afternoon	Morning	Afternoon	Morning	Afternoon
Monday	FM1	Strength 1		Speed and Agility 1	Strength 1	
Tuesday	FM2	FM3		Strength 1	FM1	Strength 2a
Wednesday		Strength 2	FM1 (change to Speed and Agility 2 after 4 weeks)	Core stabilization medley (drills from original 4-week program)		
Thursday	Speed and Agility 1	FM3		Strength 2	Speed and Agility	Strength 2b
Friday	Rest	Flexibility		Flexibility		
Saturday	FM1	Strength 1	Strength 1 (change to Strength 2 after 4 weeks)		Strength 1	FM2
Sunday	FM3					Strength 2b

Note: Although they are not shown in the table, skills and recovery sessions are also performed by all players during the training week. Positional skills, including passing and catching drills, should also be practiced in the warm-up before most conditioning sessions.

Table 10.7 Session Content for Test Case Programs

Training session	Test case 1	Test case 2	Test case 3
FM1	• Five 3 min. running intervals with 60 s. walk recovery; progress at week 3 to ten 2 min. runs with 90 s. walk recovery • Cool-down: Brisk walking, 5 min., and self-release stretches with foam roller	• Warm-up: Top-Five Ladder Drills, 2 sets, walk-back recovery • Figure-Eight Intervals, 6 repetitions, rest 90 s. between repetitions • Cool-down: Half-length jog with half-length walk, 4 repetitions, plus static stretching • From week 4, change to Running Clock Drill, 8 sets of 1 repetition, rest 2 min. between sets	• Three control drills, 3 sets of each drill • Partner Passing Medley, 30 s. of each drill • Lucky 13 Circuit Drill, rest 30 s. between drills, 2 sets, rest 3 min. between sets • Cool-down: Stride the pitch length, 2 repetitions, 30 s. recovery; static stretching
FM2	• Running Clock Drill, 4 sets of: 1 repetition, rest 30 s., 2 repetitions, rest 60 s., 3 repetitions, rest 90 s.; from week 4, increase to 6 sets • Cool-down: slow jogging, static stretching, and an ice bath		
FM3	• Cross-training combo, 3 sets of: 5 min. cycling, 5 min. rowing • Finish with 12 min. swim		

(continued)

Table 10.7 *(continued)*

Training session	Test case 1	Test case 2	Test case 3
Strength 1	• Warm-up: Control drills and skipping • Back Squat, superset of 3 sets of 6 repetitions each with Lunge and Dummy Pass, 10 on each leg, rest 2 min. between sets • Hamstring Pendulum, 2 sets of 6 repetitions each, rest 2 min. between sets • Weighted Push-Up, superset of 4 sets of 3 repetitions each with Supine Maul-Up, 6 repetitions, rest 2 min. between sets • Static core stabilization medley, 12 min. • Static stretching • Ice bath (postsession)	• Warm-up: Three control drills, 2 sets of each drill, then pass off each hand to partner, 30 repetitions • Leg Raise and Support, 20 repetitions • Arm and Leg Raise, 10 repetitions • Rotating Ramp, 4 sets • Prone Extensions, 3 sets of 10 repetitions, rest 30 s. between sets • Lunge and Dummy Pass, 3 sets of 14 repetitions with 3 kg medicine ball, rest 90 s. between sets • Lateral Wall Squat, superset of 3 sets of 10 repetitions on each leg with Shoulder Step-Ups, 10 repetitions, rest 2 min. between sets • Multidirectional Lunge, 4 repetitions, rest 90 s. between repetitions; add 3 kg medicine ball in week 3 • Core stabilization drills • Cool-down: Contrast showers • For medicine ball drills, increase to 5 kg ball when able to	• Warm-up: Two static core stabilization drills, 3 sets of each drill, then skipping, 3 repetitions of 45 s. • Deadlift (light load), 4 sets of 6 repetitions, rest 2 min. between sets • Back Squat (medium load), superset of 4 sets of 12 repetitions with Lateral Wall Squat, 6 repetitions, rest 2 min. between sets • Front Squat (medium load), superset of 3 sets of 10 repetitions with Lunge and Dummy Pass, 6 repetitions with 3 kg medicine ball, rest 2 min. between sets • Shoulder Press, superset of 5 sets of 10 repetitions each with Front and Lateral Raises, 10 repetitions, rest 90 s. between sets • Hamstring Pendulum, 2 sets of 10 repetitions each, rest 60 s. between sets

Strength 2

- Warm-up: Passing drills plus single-leg balance drills
- Shoulder Press, superset of 3 sets of 6 repetitions each with 20 Shoulder Step-Ups, rest 2 min. between sets
- Bent-Over Row, superset of 3 sets of 6 repetitions each with 5 Neck Stabilizer repetitions, rest 2 min. between sets
- Dynamic core stabilization medley, 12 min.
- Cool-down: Pool regen session

- Warm-up: Three sets of each of two static core stabilization drills followed by 3 sets of skipping for 30 seconds
- Single-Leg Bridge, 3 sets of 4 repetitions on each leg, no rest
- Back Squat, 3 sets of 6 repetitions each, lifting 30 kg, rest 2 min. between sets
- Bench Press, 3 sets of 6 repetitions each, lifting 35 kg, rest 2 min. between sets
- Bent-Over Row, 2 sets of 6 repetitions each, lifting 20 kg, rest 2 min. between sets
- Front and Lateral Raises, 2 sets of 6 repetitions each, lifting 5 kg dumbbells, resting 90 s. between sets
- At week 3, introduce Hamstring Pendulum, 2 sets of 8 repetitions each, resting 90 s. between sets

2a. Pulling:
- Three sets of 20 scrum-half passes, alternating passing from the floor and from a lineout, rest 60 s. between sets
- Bent-Over Row, superset of 4 sets of 12 repetitions each with 10 repetitions of Push-Up and Pull, rest 90 s. between sets
- Supine Maul-Up, superset of sets of 10 repetitions each with 2 repetitions of a 10 s. Swiss Ball Maul, rest 90 s. between sets
- Bicep curl and press, 8 sets of 3 repetitions with each arm as you stand on one leg, resting 90 s. between sets

2b. Pushing:
- Three static core stabilization drills, 3 sets of each
- Bench Press, superset of 4 sets of 10 repetitions each with 10 push-ups, rest 2 min. between sets

- Three dynamic core stabilization drills, 3 sets of each drill
- Cool-down: Contrast showers

(continued)

Table 10.7 *(continued)*

Training session	Test case 1	Test case 2	Test case 3
			• Incline push-ups, superset of 3 sets of 10 repetitions each with Off-Load Rotation, 10 repetitions, rest 60 s. between sets • Shoulder Step-Ups, superset of 3 sets of 10 repetitions each with T Raises and Lateral Raises (light dumbbells), 10 repetitions, rest 90 s. between sets • Cool-down: Six-length swim at a comfortable pace, alternating between front crawl and breaststroke, then finish with static stretching in the water
Flexibility	Two each of static, active, and self-release stretching drills, 3 sets of each	Slow jogging, 8 min., followed by self-release stretching drills, 35 min.	Cycling, 12 min. at a steady pace, followed by static stretching, 30 min.

Speed and Agility	• Top-Five Ladder Drills, 2 sets with walk-back recovery • Functional stretches • Medicine Ball Chuck and Chase, 4 repetitions, rest 2 min. between repetitions • Sprint 5 meters after rising from floor, 4 repetitions, rest 3 min. between repetitions • Lineout Evasion runs (simulate lift instead of jump), 4 repetitions, rest 2 min. between repetitions • Cool-down: Contrast showers	• Warm-up: Top-Five Ladder Drills, 2 sets with walk-back recovery • Stadium Step Accelerations (26 steps), 4 repetitions, rest 3 min. between repetitions • Side Step, 3 repetitions, rest 2 min. between repetitions • Cool-down: Striding over 60 m, 3 repetitions with walk-back recovery; static stretching	• Top-Five Ladder Drills, 2 sets with walk-back recovery • Three functional stretches and 3 active stretches, 2 sets of each • Sprint 15 m from scrum base to simulate picking up the ball from the base of a scrum, 4 repetitions with full recovery between repetitions • Deceleration runs (whistle blown between the 5 and 15 m markers), 4 repetitions with full recovery between repetitions • Side Step, 3 repetitions, and Hit and Spin, 3 repetitions, with full recovery between repetitions • Cool-down: Static stretching; contrast showers
Speed and Agility 2	• Warm-up: Top-Five Ladder Drills, 2 sets with walk-back recovery • In-and-Out Swerve, 4 repetitions, rest 90 s. between repetitions • Weighted Vest Accelerations over 15 m, 4 repetitions, rest 3 min. between repetitions • Accelerations over 15 m without vest, 4 repetitions, rest 4 min. between repetitions		

ABOUT THE AUTHORS

An integral part of the England setup in the buildup to World Cup success and British Lion, **Dan Luger** plays for top French side Perpignan, following successful seasons with leading London clubs NEC Harlequins and Saracens. He has been described as the most exciting wing and deadliest finisher in European rugby, having scored 24 times for England in 38 appearances. Renowned for his dedication to training, Dan presents speed workshops through-

out Europe that are aimed at everyone from serious coaches to young players. He is one of the fittest and fastest men in world rugby.

In 2004 Luger was awarded Member of the Order of the British Empire on the Queen's New Year's Honours List for his services to rugby. Luger was born in London and is currently living in the south of France.

Paul Pook is strength and conditioning coach for NEC Harlequins RFC and has worked with elite athletes in a wide variety of sports, including squash, swimming, track and field, and rowing. Pook is a former professional rugby player and has worked with many of the world's top international players. He is recognized for his innovative approach to sports conditioning. Pook is co-author of *The Core Workout* and managing director of Fitness 4 Sport

Limited. He edits www.fitness4rugby.com, the leading rugby fitness Web site; and he is in training for triathlons and a stage of the Tour de France.